2.688

4.95

GW00702773

CAMBRIDGE 1 XI 83

The American System of Government

Ernest S. Griffith

The American System
of Government

SIXTH EDITION

Methuen

NEW YORK AND LONDON

First published in 1954 by
Methuen & Co. Ltd
Second revised edition 1966
Third revised edition (American 5th revised edition) 1976
Sixth revised edition* published in 1983 by
Methuen, Inc.
733 Third Avenue, New York, NY 10017
Published in Great Britain by
Methuen & Co. Ltd
11 New Fetter Lane, London EC4P 4EE

© 1954, 1966, 1976, 1983 Ernest S. Griffith

Printed in Great Britain by
Richard Clay (The Chaucer Press), Ltd
Bungay, Suffolk

Library of Congress Cataloging in Publication Data

Griffith, Ernest Stacey, 1896–
   The American system of government.
   Bibliography: p.
   Includes index.
   1. United States – Politics and government. I. Title.
JK34.G7 1983   320.973   83–8226
ISBN 0–416–35090–9
ISBN 0–416–35100–X (University paperback 129)

British Library Cataloguing in Publication Data
Griffith, Ernest S.
   The American system of government. – 6th ed.
   1. Civics
   I. Title
   320.473   JK1759
   ISBN 0–416–35090–9
   ISBN 0–416–35100–X Pbk

* The British fourth edition is to be known as the sixth edition, in order to
  align it with the American numbering.

Contents

Preface

During 1951–52, I was privileged to serve as a visiting lecturer, chiefly on American government, at Oxford University and also in a more limited fashion at the universities of Birmingham, Manchester, and Liverpool, and the University College of Swansea. Interest in the study of American government was considerable, but misconceptions and stereotyped ideas were widespread. It was this fact that has encouraged me to write the work that follows – a description or analysis of American government written specifically for those whose experience is more with governments of other types, especially the British parliamentary system. It thus makes constant reference to parallels and contrasts with this system. This very fact may enhance its value to Americans as well, because insights resulting from comparison and contrast are not really possible to those who confine their inquiry to a description of our government alone.

The central theme is that the American government is largely a government of 'built-in' restraints. These restraints force the kind of accountability that must carry conviction with it before power may be exercised by either the executive or Congress. They also hamper or even prevent any major change in policy or direction unless – and until – a considerable measure of support for such change has evidenced itself among each of the major economic groups and regions that go to make up this complex nation.

It is my belief that in the American setting these end results are, on the whole, sound. However, the reader should be aware that these same restraints are severely criticized by a substantial number of Americans as well as students and observers of other nations, who, by and large, would prefer a smoother path for majority rule. It is no coincidence that most of these critics are found among the admirers of the Parliamentary system (I include myself in this general category) and especially among those who would draw heavily upon British experience to introduce party responsibility and discipline into the American system.

Wilfrid Harrison, of Queen's College, Chairman of the Subfaculty of Politics of Oxford University, John H. Hawgood, Chairman of the Department of History and Political Science of the University of Birmingham, and Hugh Elsbree, formerly Director of the Legislative Reference Service, have offered many suggestions of great value. To them go my sincere gratitude and my regret for such shortcomings as the work still possesses. These latter are not their fault. My thanks also go to my secretary, Miss Elsie Fetter, for her discriminating transcription and to my wife for her constant aid and encouragement.

Ernest S. Griffith
Washington, DC
October 1953

Preface to the second edition

In terms of the general theme and approach, no major changes from the original edition appear necessary. I believe that the intervening years have further confirmed the original analysis. Because of the great and growing importance of the subject, a chapter on national defense has been added. The helpful criticism of my colleagues Roger Hilsman, Jr., and Charles H. Donnelly is gratefully acknowledged.

E.S.G.
Washington, DC
May 1959

Preface to the third edition

Extensive revision has not seemed necessary for this new edition, although I have made a number of textual changes throughout to bring the book up to date. I have attempted to forecast the effects of President Kennedy's view of the nature of his office and responsibilities, but, for the most part, it is too early to distinguish between transitory developments and long-range trends. The over-all decline in stature of the cabinet as an effective coordinating body, the clarified and responsible role of the President in presenting programs, the independent and informed judgment of Congress on these programs – these are trends of recent decades that show every sign of continuing. A strong President is always able to explore bold new usages of the powers inherent in the constitutional framework.

E.S.G.
Washington, DC
October 1961

Preface to the fourth edition

This new edition has been completely re-edited and newly typeset. The basic themes of the original edition remain intact, however. The search for consensus, the built-in balances which have in them sufficient suppleness to adapt themselves to variations in needs and personalities, the constitutionalism which allows for both stability and change – these have, perhaps more than ever, found their expression in the Johnson Administration. The Supreme Court's more affirmative role and the apparently temporary association of the Republican Party with conservatism are the two developments most evident since the Third Edition. Discussion of these trends and more recent data have been incorporated in this new edition.

E.S.G.
Washington, DC
March 1965

Preface to the fifth edition

Ten years have passed since the Fourth Edition. The American system of government has successfully passed through a major crisis in the surmounting of challenges put to it by the flawed ethics and the exaggerated claims to presidential power of the Nixon administration. Recent democratic trends in Congress have cracked the seniority rule in committee chairmanships. The system as a whole has exhibited a resiliency appropriate to a period of explosive change. What remain unsolved are the problems of 'big government', economic pluralism entrenched in bureaucratic-Congressional subcommittee relationships, and the uncertain roles of state and local units in what was once a genuine federal system. Nixon did have answers to these three problems, but they were aborted for the time being.

Thus, recent developments figure more in this edition than in the earlier editions. The chapters on the Executive Branch have been largely rewritten. The American system currently faces administrative and international economic crises, rather than the earlier Constitutional problems. As this is being written, the great question is whether the political climate will allow the government to cope.

E.S.G.
Washington, DC
October 1975

Preface to the sixth edition

A massive and fundamental change in the general attitude of the majority of the electorate occurred in the elections of 1980. By a popular vote of 42,797,153 to 34,434,100, Ronald Reagan defeated President Carter. In electoral votes, the result was overwhelming: Reagan, 489; Carter, 49.

Such a drastic change was not as apparent in Congress; true, the Republicans gained control of the Senate, and the Democratic majority was reduced in the House. There were enough Southern Democrats supporting much of the Reagan program to give the new president a 'honeymoon' his first year and for much of his second year. Defections from aspects of the program on the part of moderate liberal Republicans made the working out of an executive-legislative consensus increasingly difficult during 1982. The 1982 elections extended the area of doubt.

What were the major issues accounting for the magnitude of the Reagan victory, apart from a negative image of the Carter years?

Without attempting to arrange these issues in order of magnitude, those stressed by Reagan during the campaign included a federal government out of control as to size, cost, overregulation, fragmentation, erosion of state and local responsibilities, a weakened defense, and growing federal deficits. Also included were the need for 'supply side' economics, emphasizing tax cuts and favors to business, and a stress on national malaise. Results (as of date of writing) of Reagan's efforts to deal with these problems will appear in many of the chapters.

Internal and external instabilities have multiplied since the Fifth Edition. These instabilities are continuing in aggravated form.

E.S.G.
Washington, DC
January 1983

I

Introduction

To capture the genius of the government of the United States is far from easy. Not only is this true for the British and others accustomed to parliamentary institutions; it is true also for the Americans themselves. Too often the Americans content themselves with the formal clauses of their Constitution – its separation of powers, its federal system, its Bill of Rights. Even when institutions not explicitly mentioned in the Constitution are added, such as the cabinet and the party system, there is still an uncomfortable feeling that something vital is missing.

Without doing too great violence to truth, one can describe the British system of government in relatively few words. There is the principle of concentration of responsibility, derived from a broad electorate, but steadily narrowing from House of Commons to majority party, from party to Cabinet, from Cabinet to Prime Minister. In this setting a 'government' can govern; an opposition can criticize and offer alternatives. The necessary degree of expertness in modern government is provided by a permanent civil service under the Cabinet. No hierarchy of law in the shape of a written constitution weakens the omni-competence of Parliament; no irresponsible exercise of residual executive power is outside the area of parliamentary questioning. Yet one of the major premises of the British system has recently weakened. This is that in order to assure a government that can really govern, it requires almost automatic party support in House of Commons voting, once a Cabinet has decided – after consultation with interested 'backbenchers' – what its policy is to be.[1]

By contrast, the American system is more elusive; it yields itself less readily to understanding and summarization. It possesses a written constitution, and there are always metes and bounds set to governmental action by a supreme and written constitution. Some constitutional provisions set limitations upon all government. Moreover, the system is also a federal system, and some provisions set limitations upon the national government and some upon the state governments. Still other provisions set limitations upon several institutions within the national government. Separate election of President and Congress is provided, and this separation has not only scattered power but it seems on the surface also to have institutionalized a permanent conflict between these two great branches. A more fundamental interpretation is that which perceives how the Constitution by its creation of an independent executive and an independent legislature has in practice incorporated a requirement that each of these two branches must justify its policy with the other as its constitutional equal. Combining independent elections of the two branches, federalism, and checks and balances, the system has produced what for want of a better term may be called 'government by consensus' – a tacit requirement that major changes must have the support of more than a bare majority of the electorate. Then, too, the location of leadership is highly fluid in the United States. The role played by political party, while fairly strong in matters of organization, is loose and probably still diminishing in matters of policy. The inherent power that always goes with expertness is shared among the bureaucracy, the Congressional staffs, and private pressure groups. That these various and highly conglomerate elements do, in fact, constitute a workable system, in some respects surprisingly adapted to the needs of contemporary governance, is the principal theme of this book.

The British will naturally search for American parallels with their own parliamentary institutions. Nor will they search altogether in vain. Notably in the first few years of the long Presidency of Franklin Roosevelt, impressive evidence could be adduced that, behind the formal facade of the Constitution, usage had brought the two nations under strikingly similar polities. The President was exercising the type of legislative leadership that Britain expected from her Prime Minister. The overwhelming majority of major legislative proposals in point of fact were initiated in the executive branch by the departments, the American counterpart of the British ministries. Congress, under the whip of party responsibility and discipline and faced with the over-riding technical competence on which proposed measures seemed to be based, normally confined its legislative action to minor amendments and ratification. The compulsion of the need to battle the Great Depression was an additional factor. While recent years have brought a very considerable renaissance of independent Congressional activity, it is still too early to say decisively whether the long-range trend of executive ascendency has, in fact, been permanently arrested.

Clearly the Nixon administration sought to accelerate executive ascendency. So far did it overshoot the acceptable norm that it came crashing down. Part of the restraint was judicial in origin. The President resigned. President Ford, who succeeded Nixon, declared his intent to cooperate with Congress in restoring an acceptable balance.

Certainly Reagan in his first two years has for the most part been able to win his way with a House temporarily floundering through lack of any alternative plan commanding general support. The leadership of the Senate, being of the President's party, has been more successful and even innovative. As 1983 begins, the House Democrats have announced their intention of advocating a more drastic direct attack on unemployment.

It will illumine our study if, at the outset, we expand somewhat our introductory summary of the elements in the American system. So closely are these elements interlocked, so frequently will the more detailed description of one of them require some understanding of others that a preliminary over-all view is well-nigh essential.

We give first place to the principle of *hierarchy of law* as incorporated in the written Constitution. In Britain, all law (unless we consider departmental orders as representing an inferior category) has equal status, and the latest enactment of Parliament supersedes or amends any provision of earlier common or statute law or judicial interpretation with which it is incompatible. Not so in the United States. The United States has a category of law in the provisions of its Constitution which, juridically speaking, constitutes a norm to which all ordinary statute law must conform. Formal amendment of this superior law is by a special and much more difficult process.

This higher category of 'constitutional law' includes provisions that have given to American government many of its most characteristic features. In the first place, it has established a zone of freedom, an area in which no government may legally operate. Although the clauses setting the boundaries of this zone of freedom are by no means self-defining, this does not lessen their effectiveness. In general, these clauses do whatever can formally be done to safeguard those individual rights which history has found to be the hallmark of a just and free society – freedom of speech and worship, the right of habeas corpus, freedom from arbitrary deprivations except by due process of law, and protection from unreasonable searches and seizures. For a while, it was thought that freedom of business enterprise was likewise included in the realm of immunity, but this concept has been profoundly altered. Today, the frontiers of discussion as to permissive legislation lie in safeguards surrounding wire-tapping, use of files on individuals by intelligence and law-enforcing agencies, and the 'rights' of criminals in a period of rising crime and violence.

In the second place, the *federal* principle rests on the Constitution. Constitutional law has divided the spheres of permitted governmental action into that permitted only to the nation, that permitted only to the states, and that shared by both. This is something legally quite different from a delegation of powers by Parliament to the local authorities in Britain, a delegation that may be revoked as easily as it is granted. The area in greatest dispute is the wisdom, not the constitutionality, of detailed conditional subsidies by the national government to the states and localities in areas not specifically included as national powers.

In the third place, the Constitution sets up the *machinery* of the national government. That is, it names the major officials and bodies, prescribes the methods of their selection, and assigns their powers and duties. This has been on the basis of two seemingly conflicting principles: separation of powers (into legislative, executive, and judicial) and checks and balances (the sharing by the executive and the legislative branches of powers that might more logically seem to belong to one or the other). These are the two principles of American government most severely criticized and most difficult to follow in their many ramifications. They have frequently been a cause of confusion and conflict because of an inherent illogic. They have resulted in great variations in the relationship between President and Congress, variations in terms of personalities as well as external events. Special provisions governing the concluding of treaties offer a further complication.

It is obvious to us today that a hierarchy of law, such as the Constitution provided, demanded or implied an interpreter, even though the Constitution was itself silent on this point. This role has been assumed by the Supreme Court. Its decisions are the ultimate authority as to what may or may not be done by government; what is or is not permitted either the nation or the states; what is or is not a proper role for Congress or the President. Hence the attention students of American government give to Supreme Court cases.

Yet the formal Constitution is only partially or indirectly the parent of much of the American system. The 'unwritten Constitution', with its customs and usages, has played a major role. Usage has turned separation of powers and checks and balances into something else again: a situation of mutual responsibility – that is, a situation in which one branch must justify its affirmative exercise of power in the eyes of its constitutional equal.

Then, too, the intricate pattern by which power is itself diffused institutionally and geographically results, in practice, in a cluster of usages that together produce what might be called 'government by consensus'.[2] This means that major changes in public policy are made only if they command the support of substantial elements in each of the major geographic regions and major economic groups into which the nation is divided. This gives a quality of conservatism to the government nationally, tempered by freedom to experiment on the part of individual states.

Political party is unmentioned in the text of the Constitution. Yet it has proved the great organizer. It organizes an administration. It organizes most of the legislatures, notably Congress. It plays an important part in organizing legislative-executive relations. It organizes the electorate in the selection of officeholders. Yet, concerning party, the written Constitution is completely silent.

If the British and others unaccustomed to hierarchy of laws and written constitutions would ask themselves whether they, too, do not have certain abiding principles and certain institutions which they would not lightly change, they could better understand the role of the written American Constitution. Would Britain abandon the monarchy? Would it change the Common Law for the *Code Napoléon*? Would it willingly accept the self-prolongation of a Parliament, except in conditions of national emergency? Would it think it 'constitutional' for Parliament to pass a law forbidding any party save the one in power to nominate candidates at a general election? Why not these things? If the American people see wisdom in reducing such matters to writing and surrounding them with extraordinary safeguards, the end result may, in fact, be not greatly different from the result in a nation like Britain, whose lifeblood has been its constitutionalism and its rule of law in an even more fundamental sense. The institutions selected for safeguarding may well differ – and do differ – between Britain and the United States. For example, the strength of local institutions may be greater, because of their formal safeguards, in a federal state like the United States. Yet usage operates and brings changes in both nations – a usage born of the necessities of a changing age. The American Constitution is a broad outline, the steel girders of a great building. The details are ever-changing. So also are many of the greater elements, but these alter more slowly, and the structure as a whole still remains largely intact, though the nation has grown from a thinly-populated cluster of separate states along the Atlantic seaboard to a world power.

Moreover, Britain, America, and all the other great industrialized nations have in common certain processes of the present age. All alike must select objectives, and this selection is a product of the interplay of leadership and public opinion. More and more, these objectives demand an administration to plan the strategy to attain them, a strategy whose tactics are largely concerned with continuous intervention in the economic order. It is these common processes that are the key to comparisons between governments, even more than institutions which may have a similar nomenclature or legal base. Again and again, we shall have occasion to make such comparisons.

No one should be misled by the publicized frictions and frustrations and surface irrelevancies of American government into underrating the merit of its Constitution. Its provisions do, in fact, tend to render such less fortunate aspects more visible than do most other constitutions. Its merits require greater insight to understand them. They are more subtle, more elusive. That they are present in large and ample measure would seem to be indicated by the long-range results. This Constitution, largely unchanged, has survived almost 200 years – longer than any other written constitution still in force. Under it, and in part because of it, a heterogeneous, restless people have developed a continent, built a nation, achieved a standard of living the highest the world has ever known, given the masses greater opportunities educationally and economically than any other people, preserved the great freedoms, renounced imperialism, successfully fought major wars, and assumed an international leadership and international obligations unparalleled in all history.

2

The Written Constitution

The American Constitution of 1789 was a child of its age. It was eighteenth-century in its political theory. Its details were hammered out of the experience of those who framed it.

Those familiar with the period know the extent to which the ideas of Locke had gained general acceptance. Government should be of limited scope. It was in the nature of a compact freely entered into and severable under certain conditions. Natural rights were paramount and to be fostered and not invaded. Separation of powers, held as a doctrine by Locke, had already been sharpened and refined by Montesquieu, whose reasoning was very much admired by the Americans. Hence it was clear, when the new Constitution was to be framed, that its basis was to be tripartite – legislative, executive, judicial. This had been the familiar experience of the thirteen colonies – with their royal or proprietary governors and their locally chosen legislatures, and with the English Common Law under the guardianship of the courts. This had also been characteristic of at least the phraseology of the state constitutions adopted during or following the Revolutionary War, even though these constitutions usually reflected the reaction against the alien governors of colonial times by making the legislature paramount – with resultant excesses that furnished an object lesson to the Convention of 1787. Moreover, many of these state constitutions also contained 'bills of rights', and several states withheld ratification of the federal Constitution until assured that formal safeguards of this character would be added as amendments to the original text.

Practice coincided with theory, and bicameralism seems to have been assumed – though certain of the states had unicameral legislatures. Bicameralism provided a natural and useful vehicle to incorporate certain compromises.

There were many severely practical provisions included in the Constitution to assure that the United States would, in fact, be a nation and not a loose confederation. This embryo nation had at first been governed under the so-called Articles of Confederation, a loosely drawn document ratified in 1781. Principally, it set up a Congress of the United States to exercise strictly and jealously limited governing powers. Its members were, in a sense, envoys chosen by the state governments and were not directly elected. The mid-1780s had made the thirteen states and their Continental Congress aware of the problems inherent in the Confederation. This Congress had only limited sanctions to enforce even the minor authority entrusted to it. It had no independent taxing power and was dependent for revenue upon grants assessed against the states, some of which were seriously in arrears. It sought to remedy its deficits by issuing paper money, but that rapidly lost much of its value. Many of the states also were on the verge of insolvency, although others were fairly solvent and ready to assume their share of the national debt. Interstate commerce was seriously hampered because the states interposed tariff and other barriers against each other, yet the economy as a whole was forging ahead. Prestige abroad was none too strong. Inflation and radicalism in other forms were threats to property, as debts were repudiated or paid in 'cheap money'. There was a sharp division between those who supported the idea of the Confederation and would work within the existing structure with modest improvements and the 'nationalists', who sought a drastic solution.[1] The situation was by no means wholly bad, but the lines were drawn.

In such a setting, representatives of a few of the states, led by Virginia, met at Annapolis and drew up certain commercial agreements. They then induced the Congress of the United States to summon a Convention at Philadelphia in 1787 to consider what revisions in the Articles of Confederation were advisable.

The radicalism of the Declaration of Independence was now muted; indeed, the Philadelphia Convention has been interpreted as a convention of property owners met to introduce safeguards to aristocracy and property over against the reckless popular democracies which were threatening them.[2] It was this, it is true, but it was also much more than this. Among its members were many who sought to establish a nation with the capacity for strength and greatness, and who labored ceaselessly to this end.

With fairly general and tacit agreement as to the political principles to be followed and considerable agreement even in objectives to be pursued, the Convention soon found its major cleavage a very practical one – that between the large and the small states. Success or failure hinged upon the resolution of the conflict. Of the major elements in the resultant compromise, only the one pertaining to the composition of the House and Senate remains unamended today. Under this provision, the House of Representatives was to be constituted on the basis of population; the Senate was to be composed of two Senators from each state.

Ratification of the new Constitution was to be not by the probably jealous state legislatures, but by state conventions called for the purpose. The Constitution was to become effective when ratified by nine states.

Amendment was to be difficult. We quote from the amending clause:

The Congress, whenever two-thirds of both Houses shall deem it necessary, shall propose amendments to this Constitution, or, on application of the Legislatures of two-thirds of the several States, shall call a Convention for proposing amendments, which in either case shall be valid to all intents and purposes, as part of this Constitution, when ratified by the Legislatures of three-fourths of the several States, or by conventions in three-fourths thereof, as the one or the other mode of ratification may be proposed by the Congress.

With only one exception,[3] the amending method followed in practice has been for Congress to take the initiative by a two-thirds vote and submit the proposed amendment to the state legislatures. This may, therefore, be regarded as the normal method of amendment.

The Constitution also contained provisions requiring interstate reciprocity and cooperation in matters such as recognition of public acts, extradition, and fugitive slaves; and provisions concerning admission of new states and validation of debts contracted under the earlier regime.

What has history done to the Constitution?

Time has brought relatively little change to the text of the document. Four-fifths of its provisions are unchanged in any formal fashion. Yet there has been a gradual but decisive political evolution in the tone and nature of many parts of the government. Precedent, usage, and judicial decision, together with certain formal amendments have produced this evolution. Many of these developments and changes are better left to the chapters that follow, but certain ones are best noted in the more general setting.

The text of the Constitution was silent as to the location of the authority to set up the organization of the executive branch. In Britain, this has been regarded as the province of the Cabinet. In the United States, the precedent was early established that this authority belonged to Congress.

The Constitution was silent also as to the body with authority to decide whether an act of the executive or of Congress or of one of the states was unconstitutional – that is, whether it was contrary to one of the clauses of the Constitution. On the basis of writings and remarks of certain of the delegates at the Convention, it has been maintained that this body assumed that such power was implicitly vested in the Supreme Court. Be that as it may, in the case of *Marbury v. Madison* in 1803, the Supreme Court asserted this power; and while President Jackson, among others, did not fully accept it for some years thereafter, it may be regarded today as firmly fixed in constitutional usage. Nixon, in the end, did not challenge it.

The way Americans today elect a president would be unrecognizable to the Founding Fathers. The Constitution entrusted each state legislature with the responsibility of providing a method for the choice of 'electors' corresponding in number to the number of Senators and Representatives from that state. These electors were to exercise their judgment in voting for two persons – at least one of whom was not of their own state. Votes were then to be transmitted to the seat of the federal government for counting. If anyone should have a majority of votes, he would be named President; the person receiving the second in number became Vice-President. If no one had a majority, the House of Representatives, voting by states and on the basis of a majority, was to choose the President from the five leading candidates. A formal amendment in 1804 provided that the electors were to vote separately for Vice-President and reduced to the three highest those eligible for President in the event of the election being thrown into the House of Representatives. One President, John Quincy Adams, was so chosen, even though Jackson had, in fact, received the largest block of electoral votes. Several Vice-Presidents have become President through the death of the incumbent.

The growth of political parties, the nominating conventions, the campaigns preceding the election, the pledging in advance of the votes of electors to particular candidates – all these rest not upon the Constitution, but upon usage or upon state and federal laws enacted under the Constitution.

The filling-in of constitutional interstices through a broadening of the so-called implied powers of the executive, the rise of the national government at the expense of state governments, the checkered career of legislative-executive relations – all these represent major aspects in American constitutional history, but they are more appropriately considered in later chapters.

Two other constitutional trends call for brief comment. The same broadening and refining of the voting privilege that have characterized the last century and a half of British history took place in the United States, albeit considerably earlier. The Constitution originally left to each state the prescription of qualifications for voting for members of the House of Representatives, stating only that they must be the same as for those voting for the most numerous branch of the state legislature. Senators were to be chosen by the state legislatures. Presidential electors were to be chosen 'as the [state] Legislature thereof may direct'. As late as 1789, property qualifications for suffrage were usual, so the number of white adult males eligible to vote was still very much a minority. However, by 1850, white adult male suffrage had come to be almost completely free from property qualifications. Constitutional amendments adopted following the civil war were designed to extend such voting privileges to Negroes. But reaction to the accompanying excesses and deeper underlying economic and sociological factors were such that by 1900 most of the Negroes in the South had effectually been disfranchised through the imposition of educational, tax-paying, and other qualifications. In the last few decades, this trend has been reversed. Under the Twenty-fourth Amendment (1964), requirements of payment of a poll tax or any other tax as a condition of voting was made unconstitutional. The full weight of the federal government – legislative, executive, and judicial – has now been thrown into the effort to assure equality of voting rights, and the results have shown themselves in the steadily narrowing margin between the percentages of those voting of the two races. Woman suffrage on a state-wide basis commenced in Wyoming in 1869. However, it made little further headway until the twentieth century. It then gained rapidly and was made nationwide under the Nineteenth Amendment in 1920. Under the Twenty-sixth Amendment (1971), the voting age was reduced to eighteen in national elections. The election of Senators was taken from the state legislatures and given to the voters by the Seventeenth Amendment in 1912.

Clarification as to what steps should be taken in the event of the resignation or death of a Vice-President; and also as to conditions (temporary or permanent) concerning the assumption by the Vice-President of the office of Acting President, were established by the Twenty-fifth Amendment (1967). In the event of a vacancy in the office of Vice-President, the President shall nominate a man of his choice so to serve; and he will become Vice-President by majority vote of both houses of Congress. Provision is made for a Vice-President to become Acting President either by action of the President or by the Vice-President plus a vote of the majority of the principal executive officers (or such other body as Congress may designate) that the President is unable to discharge his duties. He may resume his duties with due notification, unless within five days the body that certified his inability shall state that his inability continues. In this case the decision goes to Congress who will need a two-thirds vote to exclude the President.

As did Britain, the United States in the latter half of the nineteenth century ascribed only a limited economic and social role to the government. The original constitutional grants of authority have ultimately proved ample to accomplish a revolution in this regard, but around the turn of the twentieth century judicial interpretation regarding the sphere of government action had begun to lag sharply behind legislative intent in both the states and the nation. In particular, the Supreme Court, following some evidence of liberalism in the middle decades between 1865 and 1900, read its later, more conservative economic doctrine into its interpretation of the commerce clause and into the clauses of the Fifth and Fourteenth Amendments, which provide that no person shall be deprived of his property 'without due process of law'. It thereby invalidated many acts of the state legislatures looking toward the more stringent regulation of business, as well as severely circumscribing the nation. Moreover, the power of the Congress 'to regulate commerce with foreign nations, and among the several states' was narrowly conceived, and this blocked much of the corresponding regulatory effort on the part of Congress. But a social conscience plus a greater awareness of evils attending unregulated private enterprise ultimately engulfed not only the President and Congress and the states, but the Supreme Court as well. The steady extension of the sphere of government action already evident during the administrations of Theodore Roosevelt and Woodrow Wilson became an avalanche in the tremendous problems of the depression of the 1930s. Regulation of wages, insurance, prices, all business even remotely 'affecting' interstate commerce apparently now lay within the purview of the federal government, and the states also found themselves emancipated from judicial shackles. If the United States has not seen fit to extend nationalization or even the 'welfare state' as far as Britain, the obstacles have been political and not constitutional – products of a greater satisfaction with its existing economy on the part of both of its major political parties. Of late, the barriers to the welfare state have been crumbling.

This Constitution, which has been called rigid by many writers, has in practice shown a surprising flexibility. It has shown a capacity to fill in the interstices and to spell out in detail the broad general provisions it contains. It has had only sixteen formal amendments after the first ten, which were really an integral part of the original Constitution. Two of these (dealing with the prohibition of liquor traffic) virtually cancelled each other out; the Eighteenth Amendment (1918) established Prohibition, and the Twenty-first Amendment (1933) repealed it. Two others, the Eleventh Amendment (1798) and the Twentieth Amendment (1933) comparatively speaking, were minor. The Seventeenth Amendment (1913) dealt with the popular election of the Senators. Four amendments – the Fifteenth (1870), Nineteenth (1920),

Twenty-third (1961), and the Twenty-sixth (1971) – provided extensions in suffrage. The Sixteenth Amendment (1913) authorized a federal income tax. The Thirteenth (1865) gave constitutional status to the previous emancipation of the slaves. We have spoken of the major effect (largely unanticipated) of the Fourteenth Amendment (1868) through its 'due process' clause; and of the Twelfth Amendment (1804), which changed the method of electing the President. The Twenty-second Amendment (1951) prohibited a third term for the President – an example of the formalization of a practice that had, at one time, been regarded as established by usage. The Twenty-fifth Amendment changed the presidential succession and provided for a President's disability. Through increasingly generous judicial interpretation and through a Congress that has, by and large, responded to the needs of the times when these needs were demonstrated, the necessary additional flexibility has normally been forthcoming. How the needs and crises were surmounted will be indicated in detail later. What these needs and crises were historically is worth recapitulating.

The first test was whether the United States would, in fact, be a nation and whether this nation would survive. This was the first and greatest crisis, and in the end it required a Civil War and its tragic aftermath to settle the constitutional ambiguities and the economic and social cleavages involved. The second test was also a political one: whether the powers, especially of the executive, but also of Congress, were flexible in emergencies and capable of development with growing needs. Strong Presidents stretched to the limit their implied powers and gave the nation adequate leadership in crises. The third test was economic. Could the nation discipline its industries and its labor in the public interest? The long story of the expansion of the meaning of the commerce clause of the Constitution contains the story of these, on the whole, successful efforts. The fourth test was administrative. Could the enormously expanded activities of government be efficiently conducted? The office of the independently elected President has shown itself to be among the most adaptable institutions of any modern government in this regard, but even this adaptability may not be adequate. Nixon's prescription of streamlining the departments and transfer of many functions to the states has remained untried. The fifth test was ethical. Could the new social conscience find adequate humanitarian expression in the medium of government? Education and social services and the progressive removal of race discrimination are of a character that would indicate a constitutional framework which proves no obstacle to the will of the electorate. Another test was international. Under the Constitution, the United States both entered and left the path of political imperialism. During and after World War II, it redressed the mistake it had made following World War I and assumed international obligations of an unprecedented magnitude.

The nation is presently in the midst of another test, involving the wisdom or otherwise of types of massive intervention of the government in controlling inflation and recession in the economic order, the permissible size of a federal deficit, the political dilemmas of the varied special provisions of the tax laws, the manageability of 'big government'. These are really political and not constitutional questions, and yet they too constitute a crisis of survival.

All these changes have found the Supreme Court in a role not too clearly understood. To recent Courts, this role has been to find in the Constitution whatever powers are clearly necessary for an adequate nationhood, rather than to insist upon the slower and more dubious process of formal amendment. The Court's contribution to American governance distinguishes between short-range whim and long-range trend, and, especially in recent decades, this has been a major factor in constitutionalism at its best. To the values of immediate confrontation of problems by the legislative and executive branches, the judiciary has added the value of 'distant contemplation' to the American system.

There remain in constitutional law certain fixed points not lightly to be changed or jeopardized. The rule of law, civil liberties, a reasonable regard for the respective roles of the President and Congress, each by the other, are chief among those which the Court has been zealous to preserve.

Nixon appeared to challenge this, pleading an unlimited 'executive privilege' to be defined by the President unilaterally; but he, too, yielded to the Court in giving up those 'tapes' deemed necessary to determine criminality.

As for other matters, let the needs of the age and the genius of government determine. We dare predict that the Court will interpose no objection.

The American people have alternately been blamed and praised for their apparent 'reverence' for their Constitution. It is not clear how specific the articulate as well as the subconscious expression of this reverence really is, as regards the actual content of the great document itself. But the fact of reverence is to be reckoned with – the kind of imponderable that loyalty to the throne is in British public life. Americans should not be judged too harshly if they attribute much of their present prosperity and place in the world to the wisdom of the Founding Fathers. They may be right. Much of this wisdom lay in the very simplicity of a document that has proved adaptable in surprising measure. But other aspects were part of this success, elements from the original text that have proved surprisingly contemporary – the independent executive as leader, the federal principle designed to reconcile diversities and to make possible consolidated action in limited areas, the emphasis on liberty of the individual and stability and strength in institutions. As for the remaining not inconsiderable merits of American government in action, perhaps these may be credited to the experience of subsequent generations.

3

The Nation and the States

Many and serious problems faced the young nation after 1789. None was more serious than the question as to whether, in fact, it was to be a nation at all. It is a commentary on American constitutional development to note that it is a serious question of the twentieth century as to whether the state, not the nation, will survive as a constitutionally autonomous entity.

Early state loyalties were strong. Broadly speaking, there were three decisive factors that entered into the ultimate triumph of the nation. The first was the predisposition of the Supreme Court – and notably of its Chief Justice during the early decades of the nineteenth century, John Marshall – to resolve doubts in favor of the nation. The second was the military triumph of nationalism under President Lincoln in the Civil War. The third was the tremendous recent growth of economic and social problems that demanded or seemed to demand national action for their solution.

The Constitution could have been construed narrowly in the critical early cases in federal-state relations. However, in a succession of decisions, it was decreed otherwise. State laws were made subject to treaties;[1] the Supreme Court tried its first case on appeal from the state courts;[2] no state was allowed to impair the obligation of its contracts;[3] the implied powers of the federal government were not to be restricted to those indispensable to the exercise of its specific powers, but could include the expedient as well;[4] the federal government was held to have its powers direct from the people and not by way of the states;[5] and states were forbidden to tax federal instrumentalities.[6] It is true that the Court of the latter part of the nineteenth century was inclined to circumscribe the sphere of government operations. But this applied to the states as well as to the nation; and when the temper of the times changed and unmistakably showed itself as favoring wide governmental action, the nation as well as the states became the beneficiary of the changed mood. Broadly speaking, the United States had become a nation whose government was armed with whatever powers the circumstances might require.

The Civil War and its eventual outcome were the product of many forces. We need concern ourselves here only with the fact that American nationalism, armed also with greater material resources, attained the military as well as the constitutional verdict over state separatism, state autonomy, and state loyalty. The broad acts of the President and Congress in carrying on the war and during the Reconstruction left a heritage of expanded federal powers never subsequently to be surrendered.

Finally, economic forces tidal in their strength have widened the sphere of federal action far beyond the imagining of anyone in the early years of the republic. Laws have been enacted, upheld by the Supreme Court, and subsequently administered in such a fashion as to indicate that apparently no appreciable area of economic life lies outside the sphere of federal intervention. In matters involving wages, prices, insurance, farm crops, broadcasting, mining, business practices, law and decision alike are based on the theory that any economic act or condition that in any way 'affects' interstate commerce (and what does not!) is within federal purview. The Supreme Court itself utilized cases to take the initiative in desegregating schools and other public facilities, and in forcing equitable reapportionment of the state legislatures.[7]

Traditionally, the social services – such as education, regulation of labor, housing, health, recreation, and relief of poverty – had been thought of in the United States as state and local responsibilities. So also had police services, road building, public works, and urban renewal (with exceptions). These activities, intimately related to the everyday life of the people, were not among those specifically delegated to federal authority. But the situation today is rapidly changing. Constitutionally, the way was laid open largely by court decisions indicating that the spending power of the federal government was not confined to objectives and fields listed in the delegated powers.[8] Thus, by the grant-in-aid, the federal government was able to promote programs in these fields that quite possibly it could not have legally required short of a formal constitutional amendment. In the minds of many, these grants have clearly overshot the mark in the details of control imposed. They are divided into so many categories that the formation of state and local programs has come to be in large measure dominated by federal requirements. A reverse process has already set in whereby many grants will be combined and the detailed control to some extent lessened. Reagan has made this program one of his major efforts. Thus far his success has been quite limited. However, in conferences with state governors, mayors, and others he is seeking some plan by which the numerous obstacles can be overcome.

There are major political difficulties standing in the way of turning problems and functions back to the states, whether by the way of grouping existing grants by category into block grants or by the federal government actually withdrawing from certain fields. Reagan is essentially right in his objectives, right in directing attention to the complications of divided – often three-way – responsibility, between nation, state, and locality; the expensive expanding of the 500 grants by category. The power of single interest lobbies has become intolerable. Fiscal problems, differences between states, the danger of irresponsibility, if federal grants carry no conditions: these force consideration of the alternative of the federal government reducing or eliminating certain of its taxes so that states or localities may themselves impose them. One pervading difficulty is the Congressional assumption that in making direct grants to states there must be 'no losers and no winners'. The transfer to the states of the right to impose certain taxes will allow adaptability and responsibility.

The forces that have produced this wave of national activity by way of grants-in-aid are reasonably clear. Apart from the less tangible factors of increased nationalism and the desire for greater scope and power on the part of the national bureaucracy, the origins lie chiefly in the economic sphere. Very great differences exist in the wealth and hence in the taxable capacity of the various states. On a per capita basis, the most wealthy states have about one-third more income than the poorest states. The newly discovered 'severance taxes' on oil, coal, and other energy producers separate these states from most of the others as having substantial new 'taxable capacity'. Moreover, the federal government has used or even pre-empted so many types of taxes that even the more wealthy states and localities are grateful for federal subsidies to add to their hard-pressed treasuries. Of late, under a program of general revenue sharing, the federal government also transfers several billions annually to the states virtually without conditions.

All in all, the question may properly be raised as to whether the United States is any longer properly classified as a federation. Constitutionally speaking, it would appear as though the Supreme Court would no longer impose any substantial barriers to national legislation in the economic sphere as constituting an invasion of states' rights. As for all the other areas of constitutionally permissible governmental action, it would appear to be open to the national government to dictate or at least to dominate policy through the use of conditional subsidies.

Apart from the grant-in-aid device, Edward S. Corwin has pointed out that the Supreme Court has also updated a broader concept which had deeper and earlier roots.

By the cooperative conception of the federal relationship, the States and the National Government are regarded as mutually complementary parts of a single governmental mechanism, all of whose powers are intended to realize the current purposes of government according to their applicability to the problem in hand. This is the conception on which the recent social and economic legislation professes to rest. It is the conception which the Court involves throughout its decision in sustaining the Social Security Act of 1935 and supplementary state legislation: it is the assumption which underlies congressional legislation of recent years, making certain crimes against the States, like theft, racketeering, kidnapping, crimes also against the National Government whenever the offender extends his activities beyond state borderlines. The usually cited justification for such legislation is that which was advanced forty years ago in the above quoted Hoke Case (Hoke v. United States; 227 US 308, 322).[9]

However true this picture might be in a legalistic sense – and it could be modified, arrested, or reversed even in this sense – this general thesis of the abandonment of the working essence of federalism is subject to modification in actual operations and behavior. Even in the most traditional state and local functions, the smaller units may no longer have exclusive jurisdiction. But they still have autonomy in some measure. Their vitality is still very great. The same social conscience that was among the factors causing the Supreme Court to let down the barriers to increased governmental activity nationally has had its counterpart in its wide extension of the sphere of permissible state activity. Of the three zones of power, that 'reserved to the people' – that is, the zone hitherto largely exempt from any government action – was the chief loser, and not only to federal but to state action as well. In practice, Congress also has shown very considerable restraint in fields such as unemployment insurance, in curtailing state discretion, even through conditional grants-in-aid. Interlevel cooperation has greatly increased. Regional administrative units, themselves often federal in nature, are created to deal with problems (chiefly river-basin conservation and development) that cut across state lines. States are modernizing their governments, and as these governments grow more efficient, they may well find themselves entrusted with wider functions.[10] Loyalties to the states are still strong, whether it be Texas, Virginia, California, or any of the others among the fifty states. This is all the more remarkable when one considers that mobility to an extent unparalleled in Britain results in a situation where a majority of the residents of many states are migrants from the states of their birth.

The traditional advantages of federalism – experiment, differentiation, political education, diffusion of power – still have great opportunities for expression in the United States, but are to a very large degree lost in Britain. The story of this must be left to a later chapter. At this stage, it can at least be said that in terms of the handling of important governmental functions at the national level in the interest of national strength, federalism as practiced in the United States today presents no obstacles. The whole intergovernmental area today is fluid.

4

Congress: Its Organization and Election

The Constitution set up the Congress of the United States as its legislative branch and made it effectively bicameral. Unlike the British system, in which the democratic revolution steadily reduced the House of Lords in power and influence while correspondingly exalting the House of Commons, the Senate and the House of Representatives, the two houses of the American national legislature, are almost completely equal in legislative powers. The original intent was to give the lower house a special role in money bills.[1] This has survived only in so far as the House insists that it must be the first to pass such bills. However, the Senate amends them freely and usually begins consideration of the President's budget well before the House has finished with it. The Senate has special powers in connection with ratification of treaties[2] and confirmation of Presidential appointments.[3] As will be noted later at more length, treaties have declined in relative importance in recent years in comparison with executive agreements and 'programs' of foreign policy which normally require the assent of both houses. Presidential appointments – the small proportion of them that still require Senatorial confirmation – are now largely arranged within certain overriding conventions or usages that govern the patronage system. This system takes into account the members of the President's party in the House of Representatives and in the state and national organizations, as well as in the Senate. Members of the Senate, however, still play the greatest role in this regard.

Of late, the Senate has taken much more seriously its role in the confirmation of appointments. More and more, it is examining two matters in detail: (a) the nominee's policies in his field, (b) his willingness to appear before Congressional committees. This is one of the legacies of Nixon's stretching claims of executive privilege, and his similar tendency to stretch the meanings of laws.

The respective roles of the two houses in impeachment of high officials differ.[4]

In all but the small portion of legislative business indicated above, the two houses are, to all intents and purposes, equal – equal in formal powers, equal in their influence on the end result. If the Senate attracts more attention and seems to command a greater degree of public prestige, this factor is counterbalanced by the often more thorough specialized work done by the House – made possible by the much larger membership among which the work may be divided.

Differences between the two houses stem much more from differences in the number of members and the methods of their election than from any formal powers. Since 1913, members of both houses have been chosen by popular vote. A plurality vote is all that is necessary for election. Two Senators are elected for six-year terms by and from each state, regardless of population. One-third of the members are elected every two years. Alaska, with 400,481 people, has the same number of Senators as does California with 23,668,562.[5] In one respect, the Senators from the states with smaller population have even a greater potential influence than those from the larger states, because these latter Senators have to give a much greater proportion of their time to local and constituent, as distinct from national, business. Membership in the Senate is greatly coveted. A high proportion of its members are former Representatives or former state governors. The tendency of many of the most able House members to seek Senate seats has constituted a modest drain upon the talent of the former. Similarly, the presence of a number of former state governors imparts a dramatic and active quality to Senate behavior, less evident among the House membership. The disproportionate number of states with substantial rural population has made the 'farm bloc' in the Senate extremely powerful. The mining and irrigation interests of the Rocky Mountain states are also considerably overrepresented in terms of their relative population.

Members of the House of Representatives are chosen for two years from single-member constituencies, or 'districts',[6] at present averaging about 514,000 in population. Reapportionment among the states follows each decennial census, in accordance with general legislation and with principles emerging from Supreme Court decisions.

The details of district boundaries are drawn by the state legislatures, supposedly in conformity to such general principles as Congress may enact. In practice, districts used to vary considerably in size in certain states and are sometimes 'gerrymandered'[7] to give undue advantage to a party in power in a particular state. In 1963, the Supreme Court intervened in this situation for the first time, declaring that Congressional districts as set up in certain states violated the clear intent of the Constitution that 'equal representation for equal numbers of people'[8] should be the rule. More rarely, a state legislature may fail to act, and one or more of the Representatives of that state is then elected 'at large' – that is, by the voters of the entire state. Each state is entitled to at least one Representative.

Not infrequently state legislative decisions in the drawing of new boundaries have failed to satisfy the courts. If such dissatisfaction continues after one or more further tries, the courts may draw up and impose their own plan.

By law the total number of Representatives remains constant at 435. Non-voting members are added for the territories and the District of Columbia.

Members of both houses must be residents of the state whose voters elected them.[9] Unlike members of the House of Commons, Representatives are almost universally residents not only of their state (which is required by the Constitution) but also of their own district within that state. Very rarely is a man who lives elsewhere in the state chosen by a district – and then almost always he lives in another part of the same city. This requirement of residence accounts, in part, for the comparative local-mindedness of the American Congress.

Members of the Senate must be at least thirty years of age; of the House, twenty-five years.[10] The average age of members of the two houses is usually between fifty and fifty-five. Only American citizens are eligible – those of seven years' standing for the House, of nine for the Senate. In the present Congress, the members of the House average just under 50 years of age; of the Senate, slightly over 50.

While the federal Constitution prohibits discrimination as to voting rights on the grounds of race or sex, prescription of other conditions as to eligibility to vote for members of Congress lies within the jurisdiction of the states. The only substantial differences lie in provisions governing absentee voting, though here and there literacy tests disfranchise a few. What constitutes corrupt practices is in part a matter of federal, in part a matter of state, law. Supervision of elections is normally a state responsibility (except in the area of civil rights). However, each house of Congress is the judge of the elections and qualifications of its members, and it may send investigators into a state. In recent years, such investigation and the voting on the results thereof have been predominantly nonpartisan.

Members of Congress may be expelled by a two-thirds vote. Vacancies in the Senate are usually [11] temporarily filled by an appointee of the state's governor; an election is later held as the state legislature may direct. Vacancies in the House are filled through special elections.

Nominations are governed by state laws, and in general are made by the same processes as govern the nominating of all candidates.[12] The salary of a House member has been fixed at $69,800, of a Senator at $60,662. To these sums are added many perquisites. In compensation for their lower salaries the Senators are allowed to remove the limit on their external earnings from honoraria from speeches and articles, etc. The House retained its existing limits.

The responsibility of organizing Congress is assumed by the majority party. As with other nations that elect their legislatures by plurality (i.e., a simple majority) vote from single-member constituencies, there is a strong, even an inexorable tendency toward the two-party system. This means, in American terms, that in all recent Congresses one party has found itself in a majority and thus in a position to have its way organizationally.

The principal officers of the Senate are the Vice-President, who presides as he wishes; the President *pro tempore*, a Senator and member of the majority party who has the right to preside if the Vice-President is absent; the Majority and Minority Leaders and Conference Committee Chairmen; and the Party Whips. Certain officials such as the Secretary, the Sergeant-at-Arms, and the Parliamentarian are usually appointed on a patronage basis.

The principal officers of the House of Representatives are the Speaker, the Majority and Minority Leaders, Chairmen of the Party Caucus and Conference, and the Party Whips. All are partisan. Other officials are similar to those of the Senate.

Although the Speaker of the House of Representatives is a party man and (unlike the Speaker in the House of Commons) is expected to assume a full and active measure of leadership within party circles, by tradition and the rules of the House he now carries into the execution of his titular office an intention of scrupulous regard for the rights and privileges of the minority as well as the majority party. In this regard, he operates in a fashion similar to that of his British counterpart.[13]

Both houses have Legislative Counsel to assist members in bill drafting.

The organization of the all-important committee system of Congress is a party responsibility. Membership on committees in the Senate are approximately in the proportion party-wise of the Senate as a whole. In the House, especially on the most important committees, the Democratic majority overweighted its number of members. This dated primarily from its 1977 Party Caucus, which insisted on a 2 to 1 ratio in at least ten committees. Their objective was to ensure a liberal majority. As with the Speaker and the President *pro tempore*, the formal election is by the particular house as a whole; but in practice, these elections are usually merely ratifications of previous decisions by the party membership, It is customary for each party in either house to constitute a committee or committees (variously named, and often with other functions) to prepare the lists of committee memberships for ratification, first by the house party membership and then by the house as a whole. However, in practice, the discretion of these committees is severely limited by the principle of seniority (and by the House Democratic caucus). Under this principle, it is normal for a member to retain membership on a committee from session to session, if he so desires. Requests by new members, or by old members for transfer to other committees are handled by considerations of seniority, partisan regularity, regional dispersion, suitability for the task, and (in the Senate) membership in at least one major committee for each Senator.

These committees form one of the sharpest and most important contrasts between American and British practice. In the House of Commons, except for the committees on Scottish and Welsh affairs, the legislative standing committee is unspecialized, though members who have special interest or competence may on occasion be added during the consideration of particular measures. Only certain select committees, including the two fiscal committees (on estimates and on accounts), may be regarded as specialized, and these are specialized in function rather than in membership.

Not so in the American Congress. In the Senate there are at present 16 regular standing committees; in the House, 22. In addition each house has its party committees and three or four Special or Select Committees. These latter vary in membership and duration. There presently are four Joint Committees, made up of members of both houses. Membership on the regular Standing Committees of the Senate ranges from 12 to 29. Seventeen is a favored number. Variations in the House are from 12 (Standards of Official Conduct) to 55 (Appropriations). Its more important committees (except for Appropriations) vary from 28 to 46.

It was not always so relatively simple. For many years, standing and other committees had proliferated without too much concern for logic. The Legislative Reorganization Act of 1946 not only cut in half the number of standing committees, but also in large measure made their several jurisdictions correspond to those of the similar departments and agencies in the Executive Branch. By 1975 changes in the Executive Branch, and certain changes in Congressional Committee structure and jurisdiction, have measurably lessened this correlation. An even greater factor in such lessening has been the addition of numerous functions to the government. These were partly responsible for a great increase in the number of subcommittees. The titles of the committees have not really kept up with the increase in functions, and in the attendant twilight zones in inter-departmental and committee overlap. (See the table listing titles of all Congressional committees.)

A few of the committee names call for further explanation. The Committees on Small Business and the ones on science are more 'watchdog' committees dealing with problem areas in national life rather than with the sphere of particular departments or agencies. The Committee on Rules of the House is a kind of traffic manager and also plays an important general role in legislation. It will be considered in a later chapter. The two Administration Committees deal with the internal business management of Congress – printing, staff, Library of Congress, accounts, elections, etc. There exists also a potentially highly important standing Joint Economic Committee (of both houses), whose function it is to give attention to the over-all economic soundness of the nation.

CONGRESSIONAL COMMITTEES (as of 1982)

Senate

Agriculture, Nutrition, and Forestry
Appropriations
Armed Services
Banking, Housing, and Urban Affairs
Budget
Commerce, Science and Transportation
Energy and Natural Resources
Environment and Public Works
Finance
Foreign Relations
Governmental Affairs
Judiciary
Labor and Human Resources
Rules and Administration
Small Business
Veterans Affairs

House of Representatives

Agriculture
Appropriations
Armed Services
Banking, Finance, and Urban Affairs
Budget
District of Columbia
Education and Labor
Energy and Commerce
Foreign Affairs
Government Operation
House Administration
Interior and Insular Affairs
Judiciary
Merchant Marine and Fisheries
Post Office and Civil Service
Public Works and Transportation
Rules
Science and Technology
Small Business
Standards of Official Conduct
Veterans Affairs
Ways and Means

Select and Special Committees
Ethics (Senate)
Indian Affairs (Senate)
Intelligence (House and Senate)

Aging (House and Senate)
Narcotics Abuse and Control (House)

Joint Committees
Economic Committee
Library –
Printing –
Taxation – Chosen from appropriate standing committees of both
  Houses

We have already described the method by which the members of
these committees are selected and how continuity, member preference,
seniority, suitability, and party regularity are factors in determining
selection. This method weights the scales in two ways that are by no
means mutually exclusive. In the first place, specialization achieves an
initial impetus by the degree of correlation between interest in (as
evidenced by a member's preference for) a particular committee and
the member's competence. In the second place, members' preferences
also tend to correspond to the economic and other interests of the
members' districts and states. Thus certain committees find themselves
strongly weighted in the direction of particular economic and regional
interests. This is notably true in Agriculture, Public Works, Interior
and Insular Affairs (water resources development), Labor (which
includes several conservative members), Banking and Currency,
Merchant Marine and Fisheries. In the case of legislation sponsored by
these committees, Congress as a whole or its Appropriations Committees may be expected to introduce a corrective factor and to take a
more national, or at any rate a different, viewpoint.

Within a committee, for years the so-called seniority rule normally
applied in the selection of its chairman. A genuine breach was made in
the organization of the House in 1975. The presence of an unusually
large number of new members, predominantly liberal in their viewpoint, encouraged many others of the Democratic majority to join in
replacing three of the senior chairmen by those more in tune with the
more modern orientation. Also the chairman of the important Ways
and Means Committee withdrew his candidacy. Whether or not this
will be repeated is uncertain, but it certainly should serve as a warning
to chairmen in the future to be more sensitive to their committee

members and the majority orientation of their party as a whole. The value put upon seniority still tends to weight those great substantive committees, membership of which is especially coveted, with a disproportionate number of members of the same conservative type. Such a situation is especially noticeable in the Finance (Senate), Commerce, and Judiciary Committees. We will note later how the premium placed upon seniority constitutes an obstacle to any really effective party responsibility, especially if a liberal President attempts to exercise his leadership.

A quiet revolution took place in 1975 in the Senate also. While no chairmen were displaced, an enhanced liberal majority among the Democrats shuffled committee memberships so that hitherto bastions of conservatism among certain committees found themselves with a 'new look'. Seniority was to this extent disregarded. In 1981, with the coming of a Republican majority in the Senate, seniority was somewhat shuffled, so that no Senator was chairman of more than one committee.

Strictly speaking, a chairman's powers are exercised on sufferance of the majority of his committee. Customarily, he is granted the power to engage committee staff, determine committee agenda, appoint subcommittees, apportion time for floor debates, and exert strong influence on major as well as minor committee decisions. As presiding officer, he has great power to steer questions at hearings and discussions in executive sessions. However, a wise chairman will not too greatly disregard the wishes of his committee membership, or he will face revolt. Rather, he will seek to interpret these wishes as much as to guide them.

So great is the burden of work faced by the average committee that most committees entrust most of their work to subcommittees. Power is thus still further decentralized and specialization carried still further. Subcommittee structure and membership are more fluid than is the case with the full committee. It is often the subcommittee that gives the greater chance to the individual member, regardless of seniority. Even a first- or second-term member – if obviously qualified or interested – may find himself chairman of an important subcommittee. This offers compensation for defects in the seniority rule. Mostly, these are standing subcommittees; at times, they are special. In general, they add an important element of adaptability to the structure of Congress.

It is now also clear that this rise of the subcommittees has effected a genuine revolution in the location of power, especially in the House. Certainly it has reduced the power of the full committees and especially of their chairmen. This proliferation of subcommittees has at least temporarily contributed also to much disintegration of party leadership. It has given additional power to the 'single issue' lobbyists and groups. The 'iron triangles' or 'whirlpools', already characterizing all too many of the committees, lobbyists, and bureaus in the executive branch, have multiplied inordinately in the rash of subcommittees. Battles for 'turf' have greatly increased. Many and probably most of the subcommittees now have their own staffs of congenial experts. The subcommittee multiplication has likewise so multiplied the number of meetings a member or Senator is expected to attend, that conflicts in scheduling are normal, and Congressmen dart in and out of meetings. Often their personal and/or the committee and subcommittee staffs become 'alter egos' for the members – but they stray from the member's viewpoint at their peril. Moreover, increasingly this viewpoint is itself influenced by staff specialists on issues, especially on those issues not terribly important to a particular member.

The struggle for 'turf' is itself a by-product of the fact that at both the committee and subcommittee levels much of contemporary legislation and investigation does inherently overlap. Both houses are adopting various devices to meet this. Sometimes the work is divided up along fairly obvious lines; sometimes dual or multiple referrals to two or more committees or subcommittees are made – usually tandem, but sometimes to an *ad hoc* joint meeting. No longer can a President seeking to influence Congress content himself with contacts with the party leaderships or with the chairmen of relevant committees.

Also more and more individual members differing with the action of a particular committee or subcommittee (of which they may or may not be a member) will move and even carry a floor amendment, undoing the careful search for consensus and compromise that had preceded the report to the whole House. If his amendment carries, this dismays the committee, the party leadership, and even the President who thought he had 'touched every base'. The impression that

Congress has made on the public these past few years has not been enhanced. Members themselves have not infrequently become so disgusted that certain of the best of them have declined to run for re-election.

One of the most hopeful signs of reform in these regards is the realization of the nature of the problem on the part of Congress itself, and its search for ways to do better. Increasingly, floor amendments are voted down, especially if the member proposing them is known as a chronic ideologue or a 'one issue' person. Also floor managers of a given bill may have anticipated certain of these and negotiated a modest adjustment of the text of the bill which will satisfy critics.

But disintegration or 'flexibility' does not stop with multiplication of subcommittees and floor amendments. The phenomenon of mostly 'single issue' 'caucuses' is relatively new. Some are racial, some are regional, but most of them consist of those interested in a particular problem. Usually the members contribute a certain amount of time from their own staff for caucus work. There are perhaps fifty such caucuses in all. They usually have a chairman, a secretary, and relatively fluid membership. Some contain members of both houses. They meet occasionally for discussions or strategy sessions. In general they constitute a complicating but quite powerful phenomenon, often enhancing the role of the 'single issue'.

In addition to the standing committees, a given session of Congress will witness the formation or continuation of a dozen or so temporary special and select committees. It had been the hope of the reorganization of 1946 that the special committees, which had flourished in considerable number, would no longer be necessary. It was felt that the standing committees, with their jurisdictions clarified and enlarged, could handle adequately such investigations as might be determined upon by Congress. The number of special committees is, in fact, fewer than before 1946, but they still figure importantly in Congressional agenda. Both they and the standing committees may, and usually do, request additional funds when conducting special investigations. Such funds are largely for additional staff, travel, printing, etc.

One hesitates to generalize as to the fields of these special committees. Some are used to deal with problems in fields not hitherto regarded as Congressional responsibilities, such as astronautics and outer space, now the subject of standing committees of both houses. Others, such as the formerly Select Committee of the Senate on Small Business, were defended as dealing with problems overlapping the fields of several of the standing committees. It eventually became a Standing Committee. Still others emerge if, for some reason, Congress lacks the necessary confidence in the appropriate standing committee. A few are tributes to the insistence or persistence of the member sponsoring the resolution creating the special committee, for it is customary to name this member its chairman. Here and there, a special committee is created to serve as 'watchdog' over the operation of some program (such as foreign aid) in the executive branch. In their workings they vary almost as much as in their origin; but, by and large, they are a positive factor in the direction of specialization, adaptability, and dramatization and solution of problems of nationwide import.

The Appropriations Committees will be dealt with in Chapter 12, 'Finance and Fiscal Policy'.

In concluding our account of the specialized committee structure of Congress, readers will note with interest the extent to which it meets, perhaps more adequately than the non-specialized British House of Commons committee, certain legislative desiderata of the present day. Because of the Congressional committee and subcommittee proliferation, an enormous number of bills can be given detailed consideration. This is especially important in facilitating the passage of a quantity of minor bills, including many of the type that in Britain can command only the relatively unproductive private member sponsorship. Moreover, the system gives a quality of specialized continuity to the legislative aspects of national policy. We shall suggest its potentialities in our later consideration of legislative oversight of administration. Certainly it gives the American 'backbencher' (i.e., first or second terms) a greater chance to make a distinctive individual contribution to national policy. Yet all this is at the price of a weakening of party responsibility. Probably its very specialization also makes more difficult the integration of separate measures into an internally consistent program of national interest. Later chapters will make clear the fact that comparison of the two systems centers around the values attached on the one hand to concentration of responsibility and on the other hand to genuine representative legislative deliberation.

5

Congress: Its Procedure

The British and the Americans hold the same ideals as to how to legislate. Both strive to provide thorough discussion and consideration. Both are determined that the minority shall have a fair opportunity to be heard, to criticize, to offer alternatives. Both offer opportunity to criticize the administration and call it to account. In comparison with these three great principles, such differences as there are in procedure are chiefly differences in method and not in objectives. American procedure provides for much greater legislative specialization in substance and in detail. It is suited to consider the much greater mass of legislation which Congress has before it – a greater mass which, in part, concerns details that Britain would have left to departmental orders or private bill procedure. In comparison with the relatively simple standing orders of the House of Commons and even with the more complex precedents thereunder, rules of procedure and precedents in both House and Senate present a maze, a mystery that even those of long-standing membership often find difficult to master completely.

The lawmaking power of Congress is set forth in Article I, Section 8 of the Constitution. There are listed the principal powers or spheres delegated to the federal government. These include taxation, borrowing, foreign and interstate commerce, naturalization, bankruptcy, coinage, weights and measures, post office and post roads, patents, copyrights, defense, maritime and international law, war, and regulation of the armed services. But we have already seen that in spite of the specific reservation to the states or to the people of the remaining unlisted powers, by one device or another (such as the spending power), Congress has entered a large number of fields not originally contemplated by the framers of the Constitution.

In pursuance of its legislative duty, each Congress, in its two years of existence, faces about 20,000 bills and resolutions – a number many times that of its British counterpart. Fewer than 2,000 of these are private bills, which follow a simplified procedure. These private bills include matters such as correction of war records and claims against the government. Some progress has recently been made by way of transferring the responsibility for such private matters to judicial or administrative tribunals, but there is still need for further reform of this type. The remaining bills are public. A bill introduced in the first session of a two-year Congress does not have to be reintroduced in the second session or in a special session. But with the election of a new Congress, all previously introduced bills that have not been enacted into law lapse, and they must be reintroduced, no matter how far along the legislative process they have progressed. Naturally, not all these bills are taken too seriously. However, in a given regular session, about a thousand measures actually find their way to the statute books, and hundreds of others are the subjects of hearings and serious consideration in one or both of the houses. Many of the bills deal with the same or closely related subjects and are considered jointly in committee. The introduction of several bills on a subject is itself a sign that the time is ripe for its consideration.

The principal reason for this plethora of bills lies in the fact that in Congress the doctrine of equality among the membership is held. No distinction, technically speaking, is made between a minor bill introduced by an obscure first-term member and an important measure sponsored by the chairman of a committee and urged by the President. Each follows the same formal procedure in its introduction, printing, and reference to the appropriate committee. Indeed, the former may have a better chance of enactment if there is no opposition and it has merit, for Congress has special procedures for facilitating the passage of unopposed bills. While certain members of the President's party in Congress will, in fact, assure the introduction of measures that the President favors, there is no such distinction as in Britain between a government bill and a private member's bill. The American counterpart of Cabinet responsibility is a pale shadow of the British idea.

Sponsorship of a bill by the chairman of a committee may well go further toward assurance of its passage than sponsorship by the President.

Upon their introduction, all bills are referred to the appropriate committee of the house into which they have been introduced. A parallel or even an identical bill is often introduced in the other house as well, in which case it goes to the corresponding committee in that house. An officer called the Parliamentarian customarily makes the committee assignments, subject to the ruling of the Speaker of the House and the President *pro tempore* in the Senate. Decision as to committee assignment is subject to appeal and may be overruled by a simple majority vote. A few such doubtful cases appear in each session, and a sponsoring member usually tries to obtain the assignment of his measure to the more friendly committee. While the sponsoring member may, if he chooses, make a few remarks on the introduction of a bill, no debate or discussion takes place at this stage. We have already referred to the increasing practice of 'multiple referral'.

Committees differ as to their procedure and frequency of meeting. However, certain broad similarities may be noted. Early in each session, a committee usually holds one or more executive sessions to survey its probable agenda for the year. This agenda consists not only of the bills introduced and anticipated, but also of any contemplated investigations of problems in which members are interested. In a few instances, appropriate officials from the executive branch are invited to attend a meeting or two, to go over together informally the problems facing the government in their area of action. At these executive sessions, provisional decisions are made as to which bills are to be tabled for the present and which are to receive immediate or serious consideration probably by reference to an appropriate subcommittee. Such decisions are based on many factors, chief of which are the urgency and importance of the problem, the importance and temper of the sponsorship, the absence of opposition, and the degree of popular demand. If a number of measures on a single subject are before the committee, decision is made as to which shall be given the privileged place of formal first consideration. Rarely is this position extended to a bill sponsored by a member of the minority party, especially if the measure is popular. Sometimes the committee decides that it will itself prepare a bill after more extensive study or hearings on the problem in question.

The hearing stage is usually next on the agenda as regards a specific measure. If the agenda is crowded, hearings probably will be entrusted to a subcommittee. Committee hearings are one of the most, perhaps the most, characteristic aspects of the American legislative process. Technically, they probably stem from the rights of petition granted by the Constitution to any citizen. Practically, they also furnish a convenient device by which a Congressional committee or subcommittee may acquire information. The majority of Congressmen are lawyers, and to a lawyer, truth customarily emerges from a battle of protagonists. The committee hearing is the legislative adaptation or counterpart of the courtroom. Before the listening and questioning committee members, there appears – voluntarily or otherwise – a procession of witnesses in support of or in opposition to the measure under consideration, or, if the problem has not yet reached this formal stage, to offer such illumination on the subject as may be available. These witnesses are chiefly representatives of the special groups economically or otherwise interested. We call them 'lobbyists', because they usually do not confine their arguments and importuning to the committee room, but buttonhole individual members in the lobbies and, of course, elsewhere. Some witnesses appear on committee initiative and invitation – under subpoena, if reluctant – if the committee believes that they have a contribution to make to the problem at issue. Questioners may or may not have assistance from committee staff. Committees often try to obtain 'headliners' as witnesses so as to assure good press coverage; with its consequent contribution to the education of the public, and the popular association of the committee with the importance of the problem. Committees differ greatly as to their methods of conducting hearings, especially as to the treatment accorded to witnesses. Agitation in Congress has recently resulted in the formulation of standards of fair play in these matters. In any event, the power and the custom in matters such as calling for papers, summoning witnesses, and utilizing independent staff aids are greatly in excess of their British counterparts.

For sources of information and illumination, Congressional committees are far from being confined to hearings. Especially since the advent of greatly increased staff and research aids, extensive studies are now usual on all important measures. Auxiliary studies are made during active committee consideration to illuminate doubtful points. Congressmen may also wish to obtain information outside Washington. More than 200 members traveled abroad in pursuance of such public business in the summer prior to the debate on the Marshall Plan. In most committees, it is also now routine procedure to refer all seriously considered measures to the appropriate agency in the executive branch for comment and criticism. The submission of such memoranda is often followed by the personal appearance of top officials of the agency to urge its point of view or to subject themselves to questions.

When the studies are made and the hearings completed, the committee usually meets again in executive sessions to decide its policy on the measure. Again, its staff may be called into action to summarize the multitude of hearings and to isolate the controversial issues. Discussion in these executive sessions is usually responsible, vigorous, and controversial, but it is not usually partisan. What emerge are decisions as to whether to favor or oppose the bill and then as to what the bill should contain – that is, what amendments, if any, the committee will sponsor, and whether and when to report it out. Occasionally, a committee will report out a bill with an adverse recommendation but it is more usual to let such an opposed bill die in committee. A majority of the whole house can force a committee to report out a bill if it so desires, but this is rarely done.

Even though a committee reports out a bill favorably, it still must struggle for a place on the agenda for the full house. The House of Representatives has a rather elaborate system of 'calendars' according to the nature of the bill, and different rules of procedure govern each calendar. Unopposed measures go on what is called the 'consent calendar'. These bills are read on certain days by title only, so as to allow an opportunity for objection. Those unobjected to are passed *en bloc*. To be included on this calendar, a measure must have been reported out unanimously by its committee and also have passed muster with a small bipartisan group of 'objectors'. Private bills and District of Columbia bills also have special calendars. Appropriation bills follow still another procedure.

However, in the House of Representatives most important public bills that have passed their own committee will be sent next to the Rules Committee for a 'rule'. A 'rule' stipulates the date and nature of debate.[1] This important Committee is ostensibly the traffic manager for the House, arranging the order of priority of business and determining how much time shall be given to consideration of each item. Actually, it is more than this, assuming – with the tacit consent of the House – a sifting and amending function in the case of bills that may have won their way through a not unsympathetic committee with the assistance of a militant and powerful minority pressure group. The Rules Committee members are usually from 'safe' districts and much less subject to hazards at election time as the result of opposition on the part of the pressure group in question. Consequently, situations arise in which the majority of Representatives feel that the public interest is better served if a measure never reaches the floor for a formal vote – a vote that would be politically dangerous to large numbers of the members. Under these circumstances, the Rules Committee may decline to grant a rule – that is, to allow a measure to come up for floor consideration. To avoid too arbitrary decisions, the Rules Committee must allow a bill out if a majority of the whole House signs a petition to this effect. Yet many members are reluctant to adopt this means, and undoubtedly there are occasions when the Rules Committee imposes its own views. Two more liberal members were added in 1961 to lessen the number of such instances. Further gains were registered by the liberals in the 1970s.

Committee hearings in the Senate are similar to those in the House of Representatives. However, the procedural role played by the Rules Committee in the latter is assumed by the Steering Committee of the majority party in the Senate. Senate procedure, as befits a smaller body, tends to be more informal and flexible. There is no counterpart to the censorship exercised over the standing committees by the House Rules Committee. Nor is there the elaborate system of 'calendars'. However, the two houses are alike in providing for an expedited and simplified procedure for unopposed legislation.

Space will allow only a few general comments on floor debate. Both houses guard jealously the right of the minority[2] to be heard. In the House, this usually takes the form of apportioning an equal amount of time on a given measure to its opponents and proponents. In the

Senate, it appears in the facilities extended for almost unlimited debate. Both houses offer opportunities for amendments to a measure from the floor, though the House of Representatives customarily severely limits (often to five minutes) the time available to a proponent of such amendment. Occasionally in the House, especially with most revenue bills, a 'closed' rule prohibits amendments. Debate on a measure usually deals first with the measure as a whole and then with amendments. There is no parallel to the British distinction between second and third readings, unless a limited parallel be found in the fact of a genuine bicameralism, which allows time for second thoughts between passage in one house and debate in the other.

The Senate is extremely jealous of its freedom of debate. The rule of relevancy is rarely enforced. Closure is surrounded with such difficulties and hazards that it is rarely invoked and still more rarely carried. Three-fifths of those present and voting must support it. Hence the device of the filibuster, by which an insistent minority can, if it feels strongly, usually block action on a given measure by talking continuously for hours and days. It is not surprising, therefore, to find that the smaller body is also the slower, and that it normally consumes many more legislative days in the transaction of its business.

Both houses make use, under certain circumstances, of the device of a 'committee of the whole' to allow a more informal and speedy procedure.

Voting may be *viva voce*, by a count of those standing, by tellers, or by roll-call, with electric voting in the House. Normally, the last takes place if one side or the other or one-fifth of the membership request it. Roll-call votes are now also allowed when the House is in committee of the whole. Requests for quorum calls must be honored.

A considerable measure of accommodation accompanies the use of procedural devices. Persistent use of them to obstruct action is frowned upon, especially if the member or members so employing them are in a small minority. Genuine fraternization among the leadership of the two parties and among members generally lessens greatly the potential misuse of highly intricate formal codes of procedure.

Two or three other devices are sufficiently characteristic to deserve at least passing mention. One is the device of 'yielding the floor'. By this device, a member may be interrupted by another member for a question or comment without forfeiting the floor, or (in the House of Representatives) he may transfer some of the time allotted to him to another member friendly to his point of view. In neither house is it necessary for a member to deliver his entire speech, if for any reason he does not wish to. He need only request permission to extend his remarks (or to insert certain material) in the printed *Congressional Record* of the day. Moreover, he can request the inclusion, usually in the Appendix of the *Record*, of almost any material of which he is not the author but which he might feel to be of general interest. Such requests are virtually always granted.

The order of business is fairly standardized. Both houses usually convene at noon and open their sessions with prayer. Then follow certain other matters such as messages from the President, statements as to reasons for absences, petitions, notation of committee reports, and (on certain days in the House of Representatives) one-minute speeches on matters of public interest. With such matters out of the way, or at an agreed time, the principal agenda of the day begins. There is no fixed time of closing, but it is usually moved by the Majority Leader at about five o'clock. Lengthened sessions take place toward the end of the legislative year. Important business is often concentrated on Tuesdays, Wednesdays, and Thursdays, so as to permit members to visit their constituencies on lengthened week-ends. Saturday sessions, especially in the Senate, are not unusual near the end of the legislative year. Committees usually meet in the morning, but with the consent of their parent body, they may continue to meet simultaneously with the meeting of the entire house. Roll calls will bring a temporary committee recess. Except in the years of Presidential elections, Congress usually meets more or less continuously from the first week in January until late August. It sometimes reconvenes during October and November. Motions to recommit a measure are usually occasions for the minority to dramatize its opposition to certain features while reserving the right to support the measure as a whole in final passage. Occasionally, such a motion attracts such widespread support as to carry. Sometimes this is with a proviso directing that a particular type of amendment be incorporated or that it be reported out again by a certain date.

Once a measure has passed one of the houses, it is forthwith sent to the other house. Theoretically (and often in practice), it is then referred to the appropriate committee, there to go through the same routine that was followed in the house of its origin. More frequently, it or a similar measure has already been introduced and quite frequently has gone through the hearing stage. A certain amount of accommodation is not unusual in these matters. The second house may ask for a transcript or summary of the hearings before the committee of the original house. Committee chairmen may get together and explore the extent to which the second house may expedite matters. In any event, if the committee of the second house approves, some bill on the subject will sooner or later be reported out and usually receive floor attention and action.

If the bill does pass the other house and it is important, there are usually differences in the new text from the one that passed the first house. Even if the original bill is not the same as that which was in fact considered by the second house, but if it is sufficiently similar as to the subject matter with which it is concerned, it usually is permissible to handle it as though it were the same bill. In any event, the device known as the 'conference committee' comes into play at this point. Representatives of the two houses are designated by the Speaker and the President *pro tempore* as conferees. The Senators named are normally those requested by the chairman of the committee handling the bill, usually senior committee members. Customarily in the House, these are senior members of the committee responsible for the original consideration of the bill. Modifications of this custom, in certain cases designed to substitute better qualified or more interested members, are not infrequent. These conferees meet, almost invariably in secret executive session, and strive to iron out the differences in the two versions. What results is usually a compromise. Factors influencing the compromise include the intensity of feeling on particular matters on the part of one or the other house (sometimes including specific instructions to its conferees), the general merits of the case, the degree of public interest and support, and the peculiar views of the conferees themselves. The rules require that the conference decisions be within the orbit of the provisions of the rival bills. New matter is barred, unless it is a minor derivative (such as a procedural change) of a compromise clearly within the margin of difference between the bills. The conferees then report the bill back to their respective houses. Usually, this report is accepted, but it may be rejected with or without directions to report back to conference the house's insistence upon acceptance of a particular original provision omitted or altered in the conference report. Final disagreement or rejection kills the measure for the session. Theoretically, it could be reinstated as a fresh measure in the same session, but this is almost unknown.

If a measure has thus passed both houses in final form, it goes to the President for signature. He has ten days within which to sign it or veto it. If he fails to do either, it becomes a law without his signature, unless Congress has adjourned. In the last case, the bill fails to become law – a procedure known as a 'pocket veto'. If the President vetoes the measure and Congress is in session, it is then returned to Congress, which may then, if it so desires, pass the measure over the President's veto, but a roll-call vote showing two-thirds of those present in each house as favoring the bill is required. Vetoes are not infrequent, averaging perhaps fifteen or twenty a session. However, only in a minority of instances are vetoed bills subsequently passed by Congress.

Two or three special types of legislative action deserve mention. The so-called joint resolution, most frequently used to extend the life of a given measure, follows the same procedure as a public bill and is scarcely distinguishable therefrom. Concurrent resolutions do not require Presidential signature. Either they are non-binding and advisory, or they deal with matters within the competence of Congress alone, such as its own housekeeping and internal organization. There are also simple resolutions applying to one house only, similar in content to the concurrent resolution.

Reorganizations of the structure of the executive branch, for the most part, may be initiated by the Executive itself. However, the President must submit all such plans to Congress. If, within sixty days after such submission, either House has by a simple majority indicated its disapproval, the plan fails. Otherwise Congress is deemed to have assented. (This procedure has now lapsed – probably temporarily. President Reagan has not as yet (1982) asked for its renewal.)

The differences in legislative procedure between the two nations are thus seen, in general, to be much more substantial than any differences in objectives. For the most part, these differences stem from two basic constitutional differences – a bicameralism in the United States that involves a substantial equality between the two houses and, above all, a legislature juridically independent of the Executive Branch and determined to exercise its function effectively in such a fashion as to make that independence real. In Britain, on the other hand, the overwhelming and deliberate paramountcy of the House of Commons over against the House of Lords, plus the integrating and harmonizing role played by the Cabinet as the link between Parliament and the administration, bring into play another set of devices and usages. Differing *systems* of government thus begin to appear.

6
How Congress Makes Up Its Mind

The difference between Congress and the British Parliament and Cabinet is a difference between the diffusion of power and its concentration. The values of concentration are clear and easily defended. The values of diffusion are more subtle. By and large, the party majority in Parliament follows the leadership of a Cabinet in which it has confidence. The Cabinet holds a nice balance between the expertise at its disposal from the bureaucracy and the temper of the nation as reflected in the attitudes of members in general, not hesitating to use freely its own independent judgment. These elements are present in Congress also; but with party and bureaucracy less influential, independence is a major factor, specialization is a far greater element, and pressures from special interests are more obvious and are exercised mostly at a different stage in the process.

There are five major factors entering into the decision-making function of Congress. These are the influences of constituents, campaign contributions, 'principle', party, and research. We shall consider them in this order. To suggest that this is the correct order is, incidentally, itself a commentary upon the differences between the two nations. In Britain, the influence of party would almost certainly have to be considered first.

We have already called attention to the power of subcommittees and its ramifications. In Chapter 12 we shall single out the financial and fiscal aspects for special consideration.

Congress represents the local element in a complex national government. Its membership is nominated locally by local party organizations or by voters in a 'direct primary'.[1] Members are elected by local constituencies, often with little or no help from a national party organization. To a very great extent, a would-be member campaigns on issues of importance to his community, state, or region, not hesitating to differ with his national party leadership if its position is not what he considers to be in the best interests of his district or state. In this, he may well have the tacit or active consent of his party locally.

Once in office, he loses contact with his district at his peril. There really is not much danger of this, for the channels of communication and contact are many. Letters from constituents reach him at the rate of at least a hundred a day (or many more if he is a Senator from a fairly populous state). Many of these letters are requests for aid, but many others express views on national issues. Moreover, even from the distant parts of the country there is a constant stream of visitors to Washington, and a visit to one's Representative or Senator is not an unlikely event in such a trip. This is entirely apart from the many deputations or visitors that come expressly to see a member on some legislative or other matter. Telephone and telegraph are other means of communications from constituents. Members are allowed some travel money to and from their district, and they use such visits home to appraise the temper and views of the electorate and to give an account of their own stewardship.

This influence by a member's constituency is expressed in many ways. Much has to do with public works – such as new government buildings, water resource projects, army installations – that will bring money to the area or improve its facilities. The annual expenditure of the federal government on this type of project runs into billions of dollars. The phenomenon of 'logrolling' is a by-product, by which members aid each other in securing local favors, each voting for the other's project. More pronounced is the effect upon the member's attitude of the economic and other groups that go to make up the voters who elect him. It is these groups that are the greatest single element in the political pattern of America. Unlike groups in Britain, they do not concentrate, by and large, in one or the other of the two major political parties. Rather they are regional or sectional, and as such they are usually courted by candidates of both parties. Organized labor, for example, has a very mixed record in its efforts to deliver its membership for a particular candidate.

I have discussed these pressure groups in some detail in another work*.

By and large, what is the pattern of the impact of these special interests or pressure groups in and upon Congress? It is so complex that only the broadest of generalizations can be safely made. There are four major groups with very great political power – business, agriculture, labor, veterans. A fifth group, the aged, is emerging on the horizon as one likely to be of similar stature. Government employees, Negroes, consumers, conservationists, environmentalists, 'women's lib', international cooperationists, the 'patriotic front' represent a second tier. Certain of the professions, notably the lawyers and doctors, are influential within a narrow field. So also are various ethnic groups.

Of course such a picture is a gross over-simplification. Business is by no means united except on a limited number of issues. Exporters and importers conflict. Rival forms of transportation bring pressures and facts to bear upon the same Congressional committees. Big business and little business lobby incessantly. To some extent this intragroup rivalry is true of agriculture. Irrigation farmers struggle with ordinary farmers. Intercrop rivalry and intersectional rivalry over the same crops appear here and there in the political picture. The great farm organizations seldom speak with a wholly united voice. Rivalries between the great labor federations have their Congressional expression. To a greater or less extent the whole intricate pattern of our dispersive society has its counterpart in the pressures that beat upon Congress.

In fairly obvious fashion this relates itself to regional groupings. Urban-rural conflicts are everywhere evident, so much so that those districts and States which are fairly equally divided between the two are often the most unstable politically. Within a metropolitan area, suburbia compete with the workers' districts. The industrial East and Middle West follow much the same group structure pattern. The South is still mostly conservative, with some influx of laborite liberalism from the industrial Piedmont. The Prairie States still have a smoldering

*The Impasse of Democracy. New York, Harrison-Hilton, 1939.

agrarian radicalism from their debtor days, but are essentially 'agriculture' rather than Republican or Democrat. The Rocky Mountain States have a coloration of their own, centering around the scarcity of water. This finds political expression in the activities of the great water-resources construction agencies of the government. The Pacific Coast States are more complex, and consequently perhaps more involved in controversies involving real issues rather than party lines.[2]

Formal appearances before committees and subcommittees and informal contacts in offices and lobbies are by no means the only avenues open to the representatives of those various pressure groups. The attitudes of the members themselves are usually so much a part and parcel of the social and economic environment of the locality from which they come that its attitudes and experiences have unconsciously been absorbed into their thinking. They themselves are quite often naturally the spokesmen for the economic interests of their region. The larger and more important pressure groups are more and more endeavoring to influence the electorate outside their own membership and immediate contacts, believing that such generally sympathetic attitudes will inevitably affect Congress. Advertising and campaign contributions are the most conspicuous media chosen.

It would be quite erroneous to believe that the influence of these groups is predominantly a sinister one. They naturally use their normal allies, the members from their own regions, as spokesmen. They do what they can legitimately to convince members from other regions of the justice and reasonableness of their points of view. American high-pressure salesmanship is fairly obviously evident, but this is a national characteristic, and Congressmen have pretty well built up their defenses against it. After all, government today in large measure concerns itself with adjustments between economic groups. Then, too, this is an age of organization, and what is more natural than that the normal political alignment by party should be supplemented and in considerable measure superseded by group action centering around a common point of view on a given issue? A two-party system is not precise enough in reflecting the intricate pattern of viewpoints on multitudes of issues. If these groups seem, on the surface, less evident and less aggressive in the British system, it may be because they have found alternative means of influencing legislation. The British parties themselves are in large measure coalitions of particular groups, who then influence party attitudes from within. Then, too, the various ministries and agencies usually provide formal, though not highly publicized, machinery whereby the points of view of the interested groups can be brought to bear upon contemplated legislation during its maturing stage. There are parallels to both of these in the United States.

As regards Congress, so obvious has been the phenomenon, such evils from it have occasionally risen to the surface, that some writers have made the mistake of thinking these groups more powerful, more dominant than they really are. For Congress has introduced certain correctives. Chief among these is the realization by the members themselves of the gulf between group desires and the public interest, and a corresponding caution in acceptance of *ex parte* points of view. Against the political power of the groups, as distinct from the merits of their viewpoints, Congress has employed chiefly the weapons of publicity for group activities and obscurity as regards its own decisions. For the most part, lobbies and lobbyists must register. Such registration requires the lobbyist to disclose information that includes the amount and nature of expenditure, source of funds, membership, and names and salaries of representatives. On its own part, Congress seeks, if possible, to avoid having to make final decisions on legislation insistently and militantly supported by pressure groups, but regarded as contrary to the public interest. By so doing, it believes it is safeguarding this public interest and at the same time escaping the political penalties that would be exacted at the next election by the special groups from those noted as voting adversely. Devices are numerous: delays in one house or the other, emasculating amendments, advance assurance of a veto by the President, refusal of the House Rules Committee to grant facilities for floor consideration, substitution of another method of voting for roll call, elimination of objectionable provisions by the conference committee – these are among them. On the other hand, an insistent and powerful minority group can frequently block legislation it opposes.

Yet, so long as society is essentially dispersive – that is, so long as the struggle of economic and power groups for the valuables of this world is its chief characteristic – we must anticipate a transfer of this struggle to the political arena. Socialism may substitute values of power and prestige and security for those of money, but the struggle goes on. The American Congress is a very human institution, but it is to its credit that it has far from capitulated to these group pressures.

Campaign contributions (including those from outside a member's own state or district) have grown greatly in the last few years. Their magnitude cannot help exercising some influence on how many members vote on a particular issue. Relatively recent legislation has limited individual gifts to $1,000 for a particular Congressional candidate However, the Supreme Court in a relevant case ruled that the legal barrier did not extend to contributions from organizations – especially Political Action Committees designed to support or oppose a particular point of view. The largest single PAC was set up by the American Medical Association and doctors generally. Contributions totalled in the millions of dollars – as they did also in certain business and labor PACs, and even religiously inspired ones. Most PACs were bipartisan, concentrating mainly on pushing their points of view on specific issues. They consequently contributed chiefly to members of committees and subcommittees dealing with these issues. Organizations such as Common Cause and the Nader group exposed this potential influence by publishing lists of the principal recipients of largess by specific PAC's interests. It has been argued that these chief recipients were often already declared supporters of the PAC's point of view, but this did not remove suspicion.

Measures are now before Congress to limit such total expenditure of a PAC as well as the amount it can give to any one candidate or member. The tremendous amounts given by business, agriculture, and other PACs in the Reagan campaign have been among those most criticized – in part because they were used largely for TV, an expensive but effective medium. Incidentally, Britain has fairly effectively dealt with these problems in parliamentary elections by holding, not the candidate, but the treasurer of his campaign fund responsible.

'Principle' ranks high in the scale of motives that the members of Congress assign for their actions. It is natural for men of integrity and public spirit – and most members have both these qualities – to seek some clear guidance amid the maze of legislative proposals that face them. Obviously, to master all of them is impossible. There are far too many, and the most important of them are usually terribly complicated.

Consequently some common denominator in the way of a principle is sought that would serve as a key to what is involved. Various such principles are at hand: cost, for example. One member made his reputation largely by inquiring, concerning every proposal, 'Where is the money coming from?' Then there are those who emphasize 'states' rights', judging measures by whether they represent a transfer of power from the smaller unit to the nation. Others are devoted to private enterprise, objecting on principle to 'government competition with its citizens'. Still others are jealous of infringements on 'national sovereignty'. There are still those who object to foreign aid or international cooperation. The 'welfare state' has both plus and minus connotations, depending upon the particular member. Some search for the effect of a measure on the 'forgotten man'. Others see a world government as an ultimate goal. Many are watchful for civil liberties. Many members watch for beneficial or harmful effects on the environment. Most administrative decisions must now include an 'Environmental Impact Statement' where relevant. 'Good for business' is often a compelling principle. Almost all the members are considerably influenced by appeal to principles of this kind.

Actually, from the standpoint of the public interest, reliance on 'principle' is not too good an approach to a question. It makes too much for oversimplification. Typically, an issue of government today usually involves not one principle, but many conflicting principles – perhaps all of them good. Hence, the approach on the basis of a single principle is inherently dangerous, making for blindness in the balancing of alternatives. It lends itself unusually easily to exploitation by the clever and the unscrupulous, who can study the attitudes of individual members of Congress who stress particular principles and then see to it that the initial impact of a proposal on these members is in terms of its relevance to their predominant attitudes rather than as part of an objective and rounded analysis of the total picture.

A third factor influencing Congressmen is political party. We must leave for a later chapter an analysis of party in historical and descriptive terms and content ourselves at this point with a discussion of its influence on Congressional behavior. There simply is no parallel to its dominant and responsible role in the House of Commons. It does have the important function of organizing Congress, as we have seen. Also, it plays a considerable role in the public behavior of Congress, exerting more influence than the President or the executive branch as a whole. The President's party in Congress does feel an obligation – or a considerable number of its members feel an obligation – to see that the President's legislative proposals are duly introduced and obtain consideration. The party as a whole does not ordinarily assume that its obligation includes securing passage. Similarly, many members of his party will rise to the defense of the President's conduct and policy in particular matters. Conversely, the opposing party will seek for opportunity to criticize details of the President's proposals or administration or policies, so as to make him 'look bad', but will much less frequently deem it a party duty to oppose them. From 1959 through 1964, this pattern was subjected to considerable change by the Republican minority in the House under the leadership of Charles Halleck. As a result, the Republicans were largely united in opposition on most major proposals. This negativism in the face of so many national problems was so obviously a factor in the decline of the party nationally and in the near-disaster of the 1964 elections that, in the opening days of 1965, the Republicans replaced Halleck with Gerald Ford. Ford, while quite conservative in his outlook, nevertheless was clearly in favor of the approach of 'constructive alternatives' and 'perfecting amendments'. As President he kept this approach. At the same time, the Senate Republicans, under the leadership of Everett Dirksen, Hugh Scott, and Howard Baker never abandoned the more characteristic minority role.

Party lines and loyalties are held lightly by many members, perhaps even by a majority. There is a core known vaguely as the party leadership in each house, but even members of this group may frequently find themselves at odds on particular issues. While certain members of each party do almost invariably take their cue from this leadership, others retain a measure of independence. This independence is based most frequently on the local attitudes mentioned above (including, it is true, the attitude of the *local* party), but often it rests on other considerations, such as principles and the public interest. Committee and subcommittee chairmen, fairly secure in their seniority, are from time to time notorious in their unwillingness to conform to a party line. They constitute to a considerable extent a rival power group to the party leadership.

Consistent party voting is apt to take place only on amendments to proposals, and less frequently on the proposals themselves. Of the important roll calls in recent years, in a substantial number of instances, the majority of both parties voted on the *same* side. Where this was not true, there was in most cases still a fairly sizable minority of one party joined with a majority of the other, and vice versa.

This bipartisan or nonpartisan approach is most in evidence in the confidential executive sessions of committees, where the real decisions are made. While the bipartisanship of the Foreign Relations Committee of the Senate is best known, the fact is that at the present time a majority of the standing committees of both houses are bipartisan in their spirit and approach, especially when the press and public are not present. Opposing viewpoints abound of course, but these are not usually associated with party. Reagan's alleged ideological slant has modified this for the time being, especially with newly elected Republicans.

Why this looseness of party lines? It was not always so, as witness the power of the party caucus at the turn of the twentieth century and the acceptance by his party of the leadership of Woodrow Wilson during the early years of his Presidency. The leadership of Franklin Roosevelt during his early years was bipartisan, rather than partisan – and when it became partisan, opposition to him arose also from within his own party.

Basically, the independent elections of the Chief Executive and Congress and their elections for a fixed term have made possible what is not possible in the British parliamentary system. This is an independence of action on the part of the individual Congressmen without the penalties associated with failure to support the Government or the Opposition in Britain. At the back of this independence lies something fundamental in contemporary politics – the multiplicity of issues and the impossibility of finding a common thread of agreement as to point of view running through all of them. This is the same problem we met with in our critique of legislative decisions made on the basis of a single principle. There are too many issues, too many possible positions on each issue. Some divide men on economic lines; others on their attitude toward international relations; still others on military, regional, social, racial, resource-conservationist, educational, or scientific attitudes. There are at least four main groupings in Congress – conservative internationalist, conservative isolationist, liberal internationalist, liberal isolationist – but even this classification is far too simple. Local influences cause frequent deviations – and there are many other issues that are neither primarily economic nor primarily international. The fact is that Congress, by and large, places individual integrity and individual judgment much higher in its scale of values than party loyalty; and the institutions of American government can allow this integrity and this judgment a scope of expression that would cause a breakdown of British constitutional practice.

Finally, fact-finding, research, and objective analysis are increasingly powerful factors in Congressional decision. This is closely connected with the rise of independence of party and the counterattack on the influence of pressure groups and special interests.

Basically, the democratically elected legislatures of modern industrial states face a common problem. How can they, amateurs as they are, legislate intelligently in a technical and specialized age? In the United States in particular, the Congress of a hundred years ago faced only two or three major issues at a given session. Today, it must deal with literally scores. The early issues could be settled mostly on 'principle', and hence party loyalties could be more real. Today, the issues are not only multiplied; they are also far more complex, calling for expertise of a high order for their resolution. For many years – in fact, until 1933 – Congress depended largely upon the 'hearing', with its marshaling of experts from interests affected, to provide this expertise. With the advent of the New Deal, under Franklin Roosevelt, this reliance shifted to the experts in the executive agencies. Most major measures were matured in those agencies and sent to Congress for acceptance, minor alteration, or possible rejection. By and large, this has been the pattern in most modern governments. In Britain, it largely prevails, though with some alternative aid to the Cabinet from staffs of party headquarters and the *ad hoc* royal commission. In fact, it is the virtual monopoly of such information on the part of the Ministry and the front bench of the Opposition that accounts in large measure for the relative impotence of the British 'backbencher'.

The mid-1940s launched a further development in Congressional behavior in the form of a great and continuous expansion in the professional or expert staffs of Congress itself. This was a not unnatural result of the tradition of separation of powers, and was probably essential if Congress was to retain in fact what it held by the Constitution, a coordinate position with the executive. The findings, or at least the testimony of the experts from the executive, valuable though they were, were none the less subject to certain limitations. In general, they seemed always to endorse the publicly assumed position of the President, and seldom presented the criticism or the alternatives that would make genuine deliberation by Congress possible. Moreover, there was always a danger of bureaucratic ruts or continued defense of old points of view even when circumstances changed. Finally, bureaucratic advice seemed inherently weighted in the direction of the expanding power of national government. These were trends with the scales weighted against economy, freedom of the individual, and state and local vitality.

Today Congress has extensive staffs of its own. Each committee is entitled to highly paid experts. The Congressional Research Service in the Library of Congress now numbers over eight hundred. The majority are specialists. Individual members and committees both may call upon the Service for information, research, and analysis – but not for recommendations. Expert bill-drafting services are available in the offices of the Legislative Counsel. In addition to these established services, every session Congress authorizes major supplementary staff for investigations by regular and special Committees. Then, too, it may call upon the General Accounting Office for special studies of the workings of units in the Executive Branch and increasingly for other studies as well. To these 'support agencies' should now be added the expert staffs of the Congressional Budget Office and the Office of Technology Assessment. The total, including the legislative assistants of members, committee and subcommittee professional staffs, and the specialists of the four support agencies, probably numbers almost 5,000. This excludes clerical, police, and miscellaneous non-professionals, perhaps a third of whom serve the professionals. With these added, the professional units probably number about 9,000.

The effect of this growth in Congressional staffing has created major changes. Congress is now in a much better position to adopt an independent, alternative, affirmative policy, if it so desires. Its criticism of the executive has gained in intelligence and depth. Finally, when the policies recommended by the executive are found, after thorough and expert analysis, to be well grounded, Congress can vote for them with more confidence. The effect on the individual member is no less striking. Unlike the ordinary British private member, even a new and obscure member of Congress can command research aids of great competence, and this strengthens the possibility of his intelligent independence. Many of these staffs are reluctant to make recommendations. At their best, they are charged with presenting a total picture, pros and cons, alternatives, basic data, on the problem at issue.

Thus, still another factor is added making for strength of the traditional Congressional respect for the specialized competence of its standing committees. This confidence grows when it is realized what now, more often than not, lies at the back of a committee report in the way of scholarly, objective, thorough staff analysis. This is not unrelated to the growth of the nonpartisan approach, and the increasing frequency of unanimous committee recommendations, even on controversial issues. As research and fact-finding increased, the relative influence of constituents, pressure groups, principles, and party has declined.

Thus, the factors entering into Congressional attitudes and decisions are far too many, too complex, and some of them even too obscure to lend themselves to any simple formula. Increasingly, it is apparent that each member is an individual and not a counter in a party machine or a puppet whose strings are pulled by a special interest. He brings to his duties the environment of his home district and state and the pressures of his local party, and these must always be powerful factors or he will not be re-elected. Interest groups bombard him with their points of view, and often contributions to his campaign. He also has a code – formula, if you will – as to what is the nature of the public interest. He brings with him, and finds in Congress, the realization that party loyalty and party cooperation are factors in getting things done. Finally, he has at hand in increasing measure information designed to illumine the background of any problem and the probable effects of any proposal. In this milieu, 535 Congressmen make their decisions.

7
The Chief Executive

Of all the institutions of American government, that which has seemed the most dramatic has certainly been the Presidency. In part, this has been by way of contrast and comparison with prime ministers or ceremonial heads of states. In part, its drama has been associated with the personalities of those who have held the office. No longer could a James Bryce write on the subject 'Why Great Men Are Not Chosen Presidents'. Yet, underlying the drama surely has been something deeper. In the complicated, fast-moving stream of events of the twentieth century, peoples need strong and decisive leaders, and a nation whose constitution fails to respond to this demand is likely to find itself inadequate for the times. The potentialities of the office of Prime Minister in Britain have been demonstrated in two world wars. So also have those of the office of the American President. Moreover, almost as great achievements have been associated with the peacetime leadership of most of the Presidents of the last eighty years. Finally, in international matters, the President has come to be a world figure.

The complicated process by which the Americans now choose their President is a mystery to most Europeans. Certainly the present method bears no resemblance to what was intended under the Constitution as originally formulated. Yet the only relevant formal constitutional amendment of any great consequence was made early in the history of the nation and was designed to meet a specific and unforeseen problem involving the attempt to choose a Vice-President simultaneously. The Twelfth Amendment in essence provided for separate voting for each office.

The original provision thus modified was to permit each state (by methods determined by its legislature) every four years to choose 'electors' who should then select a President. The vote of a clear majority of the electors was required to elect the President. In the event of failure of any candidate to obtain a majority, the House of Representatives was called upon to make the selection. States as units figured in other ways in the process. Electors were apportioned to a state in numbers identical with its number of Senators and Representatives. The states prescribed the qualifications of voters. Electors met in the state capitals to vote. If the election was thrown into the House of Representatives, each state was given one vote, and a majority of states was necessary to a choice. After the ratification of the Twelfth Amendment, only the three highest candidates were eligible in the event of a house election. These formal provisions remain in effect to the present day, but around that whole process there has been erected a superstructure of usage not found in the written Constitution, usage which has profoundly altered the original intent. Only the underlying principle of recognition of the states as units – rather than the majority vote of the people nationally – has remained. The proviso whereby the House of Representatives chooses the President if no candidate secures a majority of the electoral votes has been used twice.[1]

The development of political parties has transformed the process beyond all recognition. Candidates for President (and Vice-President) are now nominated by parties in a complicated process extending over many months – or (if the prenomination moves and campaigning are included) many years! Control of the nominating process is divided between the party and the states. At present, the nominating process of the two great parties, and most of the minor ones, centers around the choice of delegates to a national nominating convention and the votes of the delegates at that convention. The national party decides how many delegates each state is entitled to; determines the credentials of delegates; frames the platform or principles supposed to bind its candidates; prescribes the rules of procedure for the convention; determines its time and place. Many of these decisions nominally are made by either the actual convention or the one that precedes it, but in practice they are made largely by committees of the convention and/or the 'national committee' of the party in the interim between conventions. The structure of this national committee and the role played by the party in general will be discussed later.[2]

The method of apportionment of delegates among the states varies between the parties and is changed from time to time. Population, modified somewhat by party strength within a given state, is the usual basis. The method and date of selection of the delegates vary considerably from state to state. In some, the party organization retains complete control; in others, the method is minutely prescribed in law and supervised by the state authorities. More usual is a combination of the two. Some states provide for preference primaries in which the party membership in general may express its views as to candidates. Others provide official machinery for popular election of the delegates by the party membership. The majority select delegates at party conventions. The fact that selection is subject to state rather than federal law accounts for these differences – and for the difficulties in understanding the process as a whole. In any event, usually sometime in July every four years, two bodies of delegates meet, representing their respective parties in the various states and territories. Amid fanfare and maneuvering, each selects the candidates for President and Vice-President on its respective ticket. The state party organizations select the rival lists of electors pledged to their respective candidates; and strictly speaking, it is for these electors that the voters vote on the first Tuesday after the first Monday in November every four years. However, in increasing measure, the ballots or voting machines now display prominently the names and party affiliations of the Presidential candidates themselves – and certainly the average voter, in his own mind, votes for the candidate and not for the electors.[3] Because of this method, it has occasionally happened that the successful candidate received fewer popular votes at the election than the principal defeated candidate. This is because electoral votes won in several large but closely contested states can outweigh electoral votes gained by large majorities in states with somewhat fewer electoral votes. Because of this need to carry states as such, candidates and platforms with widespread appeal are customarily chosen. This also places a premium on the nomination of candidates from closely contested states with the largest electoral votes. Candidates from New York, Ohio, Illinois, or California are favored for this reason – and men from the Southern states, with their normally huge Democratic majorities, are seldom recipients of nominations. During the 123 years between Franklin

Pierce of New Hampshire and Jimmy Carter of Georgia, no President has been elected who has not been a resident of the eleven states with the greatest number of electoral votes. Ronald Reagan resumes the tradition. A few such candidates have been nominated, but, except for Carter, have always been defeated.

There have been rather remarkable similarities in recent years in the points of view of the principal rival candidates. This has been in part because of the need to appeal widely as regards regions and economic groups if one would succeed. A second, and closely related, factor has been the growth of the number of independent voters. Thirty per cent of the electorate now classify themselves, with at least some justification, as independent, and a high percentage of the remainder who claim affiliation with one or the other of the two major parties are ready, on occasion, to 'split' their tickets by voting for candidates of both parties or to bolt their party by voting for the opposition. This almost inevitably indicates to the nominating conventions that a middle-of-the-road man is more likely to succeed than an extremist – whether left or right. Franklin Roosevelt's strategy was largely to effect a coalition between labor and agriculture by sponsoring the programs of each – but he never went so far as to alienate the innately conservative farmers or the influential businessmen, who supported him in considerable numbers. On the other side, in recent years, the Republican candidates have usually been men who have endorsed most, if not all, of the objectives of their office-holding opponents[4] – and who have sought election primarily on the basis of either doing a better job or capitalizing on grievances. In international issues, the Presidential candidates of the two parties were virtually indistinguishable for decades.

The elections of 1964 and 1972 were unique because of the deep and genuine differences between the two candidates. Johnson clearly was 'middle-of-the-road' and sought to build up a consensus drawn from all sections of the nation and society. Goldwater, on the other hand, was basically conservative, opposed in principle to any extensions of federal action, and ready to accept the support of the 'radical right' and the racists. Except for a few Southern states, he carried only his own state of Arizona.

In the 1972 election, the situation was reversed. The Republicans re-nominated Nixon, a 'middle-of-the-road' president, and the

Democrats nominated McGovern from their left wing. Nixon carried every state except Massachusetts (and the District of Columbia). Once again it was demonstrated that only a pragmatic 'mainstream' candidate could be elected. Ideological candidates of either the right or the left were 'out of bounds'.

The 1980 election was an exception to all recent precedents. Ronald Reagan, a conservative Republican, succeeded in dramatizing the extremes to which his immediate predecessors had gone in deficit spending, the expanding role of the federal government at the expense of the states and localities, the extent to which business felt it had been hampered by the avalanche of government regulations, the weakening of our defense capability over against the Soviet Union. President Carter seemed not to have adequate answers to the attack, or viable alternatives. He was overwhelmed in the balloting.

Since 1901, when Theodore Roosevelt became President on the death of McKinley, the United States has had fifteen presidents. Five – Theodore Roosevelt, Coolidge, Truman, Lyndon Johnson, and Ford were Vice-Presidents who first became President through the death (or resignation) of the then President. At least the first four made records creditable enough in the opinion of the electorate to merit re-election in their own right. The first two of these had been state governors prior to election as Vice-President. Harding, Truman, Kennedy, Johnson, and Nixon had been Senators. Ford had been minority leader in the House. Hoover and Taft had been successful members of the cabinets of their predecessors. Franklin Roosevelt had been Governor of New York, Wilson of New Jersey, Carter of Georgia, Reagan of California. Eisenhower had been a great commander. Of their unsuccessful opponents, almost half had been state governors or senators. If generalizations are permissible, it would seem that a distinguished career as an executive or a Senator is the greatest asset to election and, only to a lesser degree, to nomination as well. Apart from Harding and Kennedy, who died in office, every President since 1892 (including those who became President by way of the Vice-Presidency) has been re-elected, except Taft, Hoover, Ford, and Carter. The tradition against a third term was broken by Franklin Roosevelt; it has now been given formal constitutional status through the Twenty-second Amendment.

One further word about the campaign that follows the nomination of the candidates. Particularly in recent years, it has been a mystery to outsiders – and also to many Americans – as to what the issues really were in a given campaign. The difficulty in distinguishing between the two major parties will be left for later discussion. Their platforms have come to be notoriously vague. It is somewhat clearer what is involved regarding the differences between rival candidates themselves. The incumbent, if he is running for re-election, obviously has his record as his principal asset or liability. His opponent correspondingly is faced with the dilemma of criticizing this record and running the risk of alienating groups that have been aided by it, or supporting the incumbent's purposes and criticizing his methods of achieving them. His own record is also the subject of intensive scrutiny. Each candidate finds it necessary to bid for at least a measure of support from all the major economic and even regional groups into which the country is divided, if he would carry the doubtful states and the independent votes on which his election depends. The net effect is, on balance, actually unifying, rather than divisive. America is perhaps the only large nation whose major political campaign has that effect. In Britain, for example, class divisions are very marked at election time, and in many other nations, religious and racial cleavages are added to economic cleavages to create party differences. Of course, there are almost always a few concrete differences as regards issues. In the Smith-Hoover campaign, prohibition of alcoholic liquors figured largely. Yet differences in shadings are much more usual. Willkie and Roosevelt differed as to the role of public and private enterprise. Cox and Harding – in so far as the latter had any real opinions – differed in the extent of their willingness to cooperate with other nations at the international level. Dewey, in his battles with Roosevelt and Truman respectively, sought to win by minor criticism, plus his own record as governor, plus appeals to unity, plus the desire of people for a change. Concrete differences in the Eisenhower-Stevenson, Nixon-Kennedy and Nixon-Humphrey races were unclear. The Johnson-Goldwater and Nixon-McGovern campaigns were exceptions.[5]

Only Reagan succeeded in making a clean break with the main stream. At least temporarily, this has led the Democratic leadership groups of both houses to try to crystallize the issue between the parties as 'rich *v.* poor', while the Republicans in power claim 'better business *v.* too costly and oppressive a government'. There are defectors from both parties. In foreign policy Reagan has had reasonably strong bipartisan support. El Salvador is an exception.

Thus Reagan validated his claim that the tide of moderate liberalism had gone too far. The tidal public opinion had turned around and the election showed it.

Organization, as distinct from issues, plays a tremendously important role in any campaign. The efforts of federal officeholders, local and state party committees, organized economic groups, and especially labor all figure. Press, radio, and television play a large part. Ample funds are important – for publicity, especially on TV, to pay corps of organizers and canvassers, and, in certain places still, to buy votes. Abuses and illegalities in the financing of the Nixon campaign of 1972 were so flagrant that Congress has now provided for substantial and equal public financing of the Presidential candidates of the two major parties, together with restrictions on the size and source of individual gifts. The overwhelming funds raised for Reagan by various Political Action Committees (PACs) defeated the purpose of these legal restrictions. Congress is now considering how to bring the PACs under control.

What then does a Presidential election really determine? Generalizations are exceedingly difficult. Certainly, the necessity of periodic accountability itself is an enormously important influence. So also is the concentration of attention on national issues and national welfare, even though it is difficult at times to distinguish between points of view. A few issues are apparently decided, though the Presidential election is anything but a precision instrument in this regard. Perhaps its greatest contribution is the virtual necessity that *both parties* nominate candidates substantially in accord with the then current state of public opinion if they are to have a chance at victory. The movement of this opinion is tidal or cumulative in nature, a phenomenon of the government by consensus that is characteristic of the United States.

Removal of a President and other high officials is by impeachment, and only on grounds of treason, bribery, or other high crimes and misdemeanors. No President has ever been so removed. President Andrew Johnson's impeachment failed by one vote. Faced with the near-certainty that he would be impeached, President Nixon chose to resign. Power to impeach rests with the House of Representatives and is by majority vote. The Senate, with the Chief Justice of the Supreme Court presiding, tries the case. It requires a two-thirds vote by the Senate for conviction. Punishment by this process is confined to removal from office and disqualification, but the convicted party is also liable to subsequent trial under ordinary judicial procedure. Two federal judges with life tenure have been removed by the impeachment process.

The Vice-President is nominated and elected by the same process as the President. During the life of the President, his only constitutional duty is to preside over the Senate and vote in case of a tie. Recent Presidents have made the Vice-President a member of their Cabinet and assigned other duties. Until recently, the office more or less committed its incumbent to a measure of obscurity and impotence, except under the all-important contingency that is its justification. Continuity of office and policy made possible by Vice-Presidential succession was never more strikingly demonstrated than in the accession of President Lyndon Johnson. In the event that both the President and Vice-President die during the four-year term, the duties of President fall upon a successor who has been previously designated by an ordinary Act of Congress. At present it is the Speaker of the House who is 'next in line' if the Vice-President dies. He is followed by the President *pro tempore* of the Senate and members of the cabinet, in order of rank.

This provision is considerably modified by the Twenty-fifth Amendment. In the event of a vacancy in the Vice-Presidency, the President is authorized to nominate a successor. He must then be confirmed by a majority vote in both houses of Congress to enter the Office.

Once he is elected, the powers and influence of a President are enormous, certainly exceeding those of a British Prime Minister. The Constitution itself deals largely in generalities, stating, for example, that 'the Executive power shall be vested in a President'. He is given power to appoint officials, but with the advice and consent of the Senate, except in so far as Congress might give him exclusive power in this regard. He can require opinions of these officers. He is charged with the faithful execution of the laws, and with informing Congress as to the state of the union. He can also recommend legislation. He can call Congress into special session. He can veto legislation. He can conclude treaties, two-thirds of the Senate concurring; he is commander-in-chief of the armed services; he can pardon offenders against federal laws, except in cases of impeachment.

Armed with these general and specific powers, Presidents have made the office what it is today. A Supreme Court, only occasionally resisting, has, on the whole, looked with tolerant eyes upon the aggrandizement of the office. The story of this aggrandizement is one of the great epics of government – an adaptation of the Constitution to social forces, dramatized by the personalities of those incumbents who have played the major role. Early in the history of the republic, Presidents Washington and Jefferson established certain precedents in the generous interpretations of their powers. In the case of Jefferson, this was all the more remarkable because, prior to taking office, he had been a leading exponent of a limited view of the office. Each did not hesitate to initiate or recommend legislation. Washington assumed he was master of his own official family (the Cabinet), and Congress eventually concurred. The President established himself as the sole vehicle of communication with foreign governments. President Washington, in the Whisky Rebellion, established the responsibility of his office for suppression of domestic disorder – rejecting the possible alternative of the state governments or even of Congress. President Jefferson persuaded himself that the silence of the Constitution on the annexation of foreign territories constituted no barrier in the negotiation of a treaty with France that added Louisiana to the United States.

The next major step forward is associated with President Jackson and the emergence of sharply defined political parties. Political parties were the principal factor in bringing in the *de facto* direct election of the President by the people, which gave to the office the standing and power associated with a popular mandate. The President, from then on, ordinarily assumed the status of the leader of the party that elected him, and this gave him further power. Along with this came the great extension of the 'spoils system' of partisan appointments to federal offices, offering the President the opportunity to build up personal loyalties and power. President Jackson also was closely associated with the use of the veto power over legislation on policy grounds. Previously, it had been more or less assumed that the use of the veto was to be confined to measures of doubtful constitutionality. As a vigorous law enforcer, Jackson also made his mark.

President Lincoln united his power as enforcer of laws with his power as commander-in-chief and pushed out the frontiers of Presidential power still further. He blockaded ports, called for volunteers, summoned the state militia, under martial law created new offences and suspended habeas corpus, excluded certain publications from the mails, and freed the slaves – all without prior Congressional action or judicial reverse.[6]

With the advent of the twentieth century, the expansion of government intervention in economic life contributed still further to the growth of the Presidential office. Under the strong Presidencies of Theodore Roosevelt and Woodrow Wilson, the need for 'delegated legislation' began to be met. This need eventually resulted in a transfer to the executive of powers of continuous intervention in the economic life of the country. Much of this delegation, it is true, was to semi-independent commissions, but much of it also was to departments and agencies directly administered by the President.

Under Franklin Roosevelt, the growing specialized nature of legislation resulted in what proved to be a temporary monopoly of the necessary expertise – a factor that, for the time being, still further enhanced the influence of the office. More clearly associated with Roosevelt, however, was the doctrine of crisis leadership, whereby government was largely transformed into a series of 'action programs', consisting of broad grants of power in critical areas and followed by drastic and far-reaching executive effort. The situation was such that the people sought strong leadership and responded to a dramatic popular appeal.

World War II and the succession of international crises that followed it still further expanded Presidential power and influence under both Roosevelt and Truman. Roosevelt traded destroyers for naval bases. In secret agreements at Yalta and elsewhere, the fates of other peoples were largely determined. Troops were ordered to fight in Korea, without a declaration of war, as a 'police action' to carry out our obligations under the United Nations Charter. The question of whether a President may, of his own volition, permanently station troops in Europe is still not settled constitutionally. The present juridical metes and bounds of Presidential power were, however, exceeded by President Truman when he seized the steel mills without Congressional authorization, in order to prevent a strike at a time of world crisis. However, the strong leadership given by Truman in the Marshall Plan and the technical aid program and in Korea showed no diminution of the scope of the office, even though Eisenhower took a more conservative view. Kennedy operated in the Roosevelt-Truman pattern. Lyndon Johnson functioned in a style all his own, bringing the art and craft of persuasion to a summit.[7]

In this survey of the brief record of the growing power of the President, a few rather obvious comments are in order. By and large, the Constitution has adapted itself to contemporary trends and demands for strong leadership and administration. Congress has delegated powers. The Supreme Court has been increasingly sympathetic. The really decisive element has been a flexible usage generated by the social forces of the day. There has been and is, to some extent, still a danger that the technical competence necessary to governance of the present day may bring its own type of 'dictatorship', but Congress has, for the time being, fended this off with staff aids of its own. Moreover, the office of President has become highly personalized, perhaps dangerously so under certain conceivable circumstances. The Supreme Court, in its decision on the steel seizure case, seems aware of this, and is evidently taking a line with an eye to future dangers. By forcing Nixon to surrender the relevant tapes on court order, the Supreme Court curbed the dangers of excessive assertion of 'executive privilege'.

The parallels to the growth in the power and prestige of the Prime Minister are obvious. The present age requires drama to focus attention on issues; and the President gives this in full measure. It requires leadership and integration; and here, too, the office seems to be adequate in its adaptation.

But the President is also the head of the state, the only human parallel to the ceremonial role of the British monarch in promoting the larger, unifying loyalties. The flag and the Constitution assume much of the Queen's symbolic role; but the President, in spite of the controversy that swirls about his election and his policies, does not fare too badly in this regard either. The people have shown a surprising sophistication in identifying and respecting this particular role – and in resenting a President's misuse of it for partisan purposes.

The American people believe that the office has served them well. Only minor suggestions for change are heard, and usually these have little support. The anachronism of the electoral college system calls for some alteration, but in suggestions for alteration, an anxiety to retain the values of election by the state units is usually expressed. A regularization of the nominating process, whereby there would be greater opportunity for popular expression in the selection of candidates, has considerable support. Anxiety at the growth of a residual or indeterminate executive power has been somewhat allayed by the Court decisions on the seizure of the steel industry and the surrender of the tapes for court use. Limitation of a President to a single term of six years has desultory support. A more drastic amendment looking toward an imitation of the British parliamentary system has virtually no advocates outside of a few political scientists. The theory that only Congress represents the people is scarcely tenable when one considers the tremendous impact that popular election of the President has upon his own and the people's concept of the office.

It is fitting to close by focusing on the President's international role:

The crucial, indispensable contribution which the President can make to the conduct of our foreign affairs is to enter fully into his office, to use its powers and accept its responsibilities, to lead a people who are capable of responding to the obligations of citizenship. . . . The President must prepare himself for those solemn moments when, after all the advice is in from every quarter, he must ascend his lonely pinnacle and decide what he must do. There are such moments, when the whole world holds its breath and our fate is in his hands. Then every fragment of his experience, all that he has read and learned, his understanding of his own nation and of the world about him, his faith, conscience, and courage are brought to bear.[8]

8
The Presidency

In most treatises on American government, it has been customary to deal with the executive arm as a unit in the triology of legislative, executive, and judicial. This threefold division is itself becoming much less meaningful than it once was – if for no other reason than an appreciation that the text of the Constitution itself assigned legislative, and even judicial, roles to the President, and gave Congress very considerable administrative powers. More recently, there has been a deeper understanding of the process of government itself which has cast serious doubt upon the theoretical correctness, as well as the continued usefulness, of these categories. Processes such as leadership, adoption of objectives, adjustment among economic groups, and planning may well be more meaningful.

Within the American executive, it is useful to focus attention upon two reasonably distinct aspects – the Presidency and the bureaucracy. The former includes those agencies directly associated with the President in an over-all planning and control; the latter is made up of the several departments and agencies concerned with specific aspects of the nation's life. A useful parallel to much – but by no means all – of what is included in the Presidency is known in Britain as Treasury Control.

Institutions such as the Presidency play the major role in the success, or even the possibility, of 'big government' as we know it today. The essential elements are obviously fiscal policy, including control of expenditure, taxation, and the use of these to accomplish social ends; the closely related function of economic planning; coordination of agencies; personnel policies; liaison with the legislature and the public;

administrative organization; investigations of the sphere of advisable government operations – or, more simply, planning and control. Planning is both long-range and short-range.

We pause at this point to give a brief picture of the present magnitude of the American national government. Directly employed are almost three million civilians and two million in the armed services. Expenditures, even with cuts, reached 760 billion in fiscal year 1983 (beginning 1 October 1982). There are between 200 and 500 bureaus in the federal government (according to the method of counting), of which about sixty-five report directly to the President. It is also significant that the government now owns one third of the land surface of the nation, though most of the land thus owned is forest, grazing, tundra, and desert. Almost half of it is in Alaska. In many of the states, the number of resident federal employees exceeds those of the state government.

How far and by what means does the President control or direct this vast organization, and at the same time fulfil his other functions as leader of the nation and of his party? The recent growth in size and effectiveness of the agencies immediately associated with the President, to which we have applied the collective term 'the Presidency', is, by all odds, the most significant development in this regard.

The Cabinet, made up of the department heads and the heads of a few of the principal agencies, definitely has grown less effective in its collective capacity over the past hundred years. Meetings are all in secret 'executive session', and very little leaks out to the public concerning their agenda. In general, the President may toss a problem or two to the group for discussion, or one or more members may have items that they themselves wish to bring up. It seems clear that the Cabinet is no longer the instrument it once was for consideration and adoption of major policies. There is not the time; the individual members are far too harassed or overwhelmed with the business of their several agencies to give much serious attention to the problems of others. Reagan has declared his intention of referring inter-departmental problems to *ad hoc* Cabinet committees of two or more department heads. Six were made semi-permanent, but like the Cabinet itself they are increasingly by-passed. Yet the British Cabinet, unlike its American counterpart, retains, perhaps in enhanced form, its earlier tremendous importance and its collective responsibility.

Most of the units of the Presidency are located in what is known as the Executive Office of the President. Of great and growing importance is the immediate White House staff. Since 1939, when the President was authorized to employ six assistants to serve in part as his 'eyes and ears', the number grew to about 200 under Eisenhower, 250 under Kennedy and Johnson, and 500 under Nixon, Ford, Carter, and Reagan. Reagan claims a reduction, but in many instances to date, he has borrowed additional staff from the departments. This may or may not continue. Until recently, theoretically these men had no substantive power. The overt delegation of power really dates from Califano under Johnson, to whom the latter, preoccupied with Viet Nam, gave virtual control over domestic matters. Nixon went even further, assigning surrogate powers to Haldeman, Ehrlichman, Kissinger, and Ash (who was also Director of the Office of Management and Budget). Only the really 'inner' and important members of the Cabinet had much if any direct access to the President.

There was evolution in this development under Nixon. During his first term, he wanted to handle the important planning and decisions in foreign policy himself. To assist him, he named Henry Kissinger his Assistant for National Security Affairs, and gave him a substantial White House staff. In conjunction with this, he stepped up the activity of the National Security Council.[1]

Because of its success, together with the relative failure of Cabinet meetings to operate successfully, Nixon created a Domestic Council to play a role somewhat similar to that traditionally assigned to the Cabinet. As President, he assumed its chairmanship. Its members were the members of the Cabinet (except for State and Defense) together with the Vice President and a few heads of the more important non-Cabinet agencies. He also gave it what was intended to be a permanent, non-partisan staff under John Ehrlichman, members of which were assigned to inter-departmental committees on an *ad hoc* basis. Earlier inter-departmental committees had more or less failed in their co-operative and controversy-solving efforts. With the assignment to such committees of neutral but professional staff, more could be expected. However, most of what had been hoped for from the Domestic Council was at least temporarily aborted as the Watergate scandals moved to the center of attention. The precise role of the Domestic Council (name changed by Carter to Domestic Policy Staff) was uncertain under Ford and Carter, and is still uncertain under Reagan. The last named has, however, significantly increased the role of the Office of Management and Budget.

Most recent Presidents have included in their White House staffs other specialists – press secretaries, speech writers, Congressional liaison men, personnel specialists, to mention a few. Such specializations did not mean that there were not also lineal successors to the original intent – men to whom a President could assign investigations of problems in one or more departments, men who would follow through to see that a President's directives were actually carried out.

Of all the Executive Office institutions, the most far-reaching and effective had been the Bureau of the Budget. However, with the formation of the Domestic Council, it was converted into the Office of Management and Budget, adding some emphasis on management. It still assembled the President's budget. Under Reagan thus far the Budget has been spectacularly paramount under Stockman's leadership as Director. A head for the Management unit has now been appointed and this unit activated. He bears the title of Associate Director for Management of OMB. Some of his initial steps are: formation of a council of the Assistant Directors (for management) of the Departments, and a council of the Inspectors General to exchange ideas and for orientation; working toward uniformity in accounting; activating the collection of the huge debts (many billions) owing the government.

Akin to the Office of Management and Budget in potential, though by no means in actual, importance is the Council of Economic Advisers. This body is charged with the responsibility of recommending to the President such policies as, in its opinion, will keep the economy of the nation sound and growing. To perform this function, it maintains a small but highly effective staff of analysts. The President, on the basis of the Council's recommendations, not only may make such policy decisions as he sees fit within the executive branch, but also sends to Congress for its guidance a message containing his findings and recommendations. This is, in turn, referred to the Congressional Joint Economic Committee, which then subjects the material to further analysis with the assistance of its own independent staff. This Committee then recommends such steps as it sees fit to promote the indicated Congressional action. Thus far, the Council has not noticeably succeeded in integrating its work with the President and the departments although Kennedy made a determined effort toward this goal. Reagan appointed persons who supported 'supply side' economic orientation. Its first chairman, Murray Weidenbaum (recently resigned), had been among his close economic advisers during his campaign and the transitional period.

Within the Presidency, certain commissions and task forces are created from time to time to study emerging problems. These are usually made up of leading citizens from appropriate walks of life, and they form an obvious American parallel to the British Royal Commissions. Customarily, their staff work is quite generously financed from a special fund allocated the President for such purposes, but not specifically earmarked in advance. Recent notable commissions include ones on adequacy of defense, the aging, the overall organization of the Executive Branch. Reagan named a special task force to study possible revisions in the Social Security program. These task forces represent a 'growing edge' of government; their functions are not sharply distinguished from the more numerous investigations conducted by Congress through its standing or special committees, or investigations conducted by the regularly established departments and agencies. Occasionally, one of these is given permanent status as an independent agency – for example, the Advisory Commission on Intergovernmental Relations.

From time to time certain agencies are assigned to the Executive Office, so as to give them a greater measure of prestige, or because the President wishes to give them special attention. At present, the Council on Environmental Quality, the Office of Policy Development, the Office of Science and Technology, and the Office of the US Trade Representative are among these. Their number and nature are constantly changing.

It is proper also to include in the Presidency certain other agencies, even though their juridical status places them less immediately under Presidential control. Important planning and administrative functions, for example, are located in the Treasury and the Board of Governors of the Federal Reserve System. The Treasury has the responsibility for formulating the tax and financing programs of the government, and the management of the debt – subject to overriding by Congress, especially as regards taxation. The Federal Reserve System deals with banking and credit, including interest rates and the 'quantity of money'. It has a semi-independent status, though its Board of Governors is appointed by the President. The views of the two are often in conflict, and the President must then intervene. The formulation and administration of federal personnel policies lie presumably with the Office of Personnel Management and the Merit System Protection Board. These two agencies operate with a large degree of independence. Their relationship with the appropriate committees of Congress is naturally very close, for the latter handle legislation in this field.[2]

Note should also be taken of the General Services Administration, which has absorbed many previously scattered functions belonging in this general category, such as purchasing, leasing, archives, and part of construction. Its head is appointed by the President.

Audit and accounting are the province of the General Accounting Office, an agency completely independent of the executive and regarded by Congress as part of the legislative branch. This arrangement is frequently criticized as illogical, but thus far it has withstood attack, largely because Congress believes it to be an efficient and unbiased instrument of control as regards legality of expenditure and a source of responsible evaluation of the bureaucracy. It is supposed to approve all internal departmental and agency systems, but has not been able to keep up with the frequent changes.

It is certain that the Presidency in general and the Office of the President as its principal constituent unit will prove a fluid and growing part of government. So vital are the functions to be performed, so great is the penalty if they are performed poorly that the success or failure of big government itself may well depend upon its effectiveness. No one man – be he President, Prime Minister, or dictator – can himself direct or control the government of a modern industrial nation. What is not so clearly appreciated is that no Cabinet made up of heads of agencies can do so either. It is clear that much of the future of government is wrapped up with the institutionalizing of certain over-all functions affecting all the 'ordinary' agencies – functions that a committee of those affected is ill-suited to perform because of the preoccupations of its membership and their vested interests in their own agencies, not to mention the frequently all-important time factor. The functions of economical and efficient management, of a reasonable uniformity in matters such as personnel and purchasing, of integration of policy, of planning as to objectives, of fiscal matters with far-reaching effects upon the nation's general economy, of accounting and administrative analysis as tools of management, of public understanding, of inter-departmental conflict and cooperation – these are matters that cannot be left wholly, and probably in most instances not even primarily, to the several departments, even within their own spheres of responsibility. They demand some measure of central handling – the extension of the power of the chief executive through its institutionalization in the exercise of his major functions of direction, coordination, evaluation, and planning.[3]

From time to time suggestions are responsibly made that the President needs still more help, especially as an administrator. More than the members of his Cabinet are needed. Nixon delegated authority in certain inter-departmental problems. These included such matters as planning, field office councils (with chairmen to guide them). Delegations to Ehrlichman, Haldeman, and Kissinger were never quite certain as to boundaries, but included the staff of the Domestic Council and much of the agenda of the National Security Council. Milton Eisenhower went so far as to recommend the creation of two Executive Vice-Presidents, one for domestic and one for foreign affairs.

Congress likewise takes an interest in these over-all functions. This is emphatically true of the Appropriations and Budget Committees, the Joint Economic Committee, and the Finance and Ways and Means Committees. Only to a degree less are they also the concern of the Committees on Government Operation, Governmental Affairs, and Post Office and Civil Service. The relationships between these committees and corresponding units in the Presidency are increasingly cordial, lending at least some color to the view that the real lines are drawn in the American Government between the Presidency and these committees on the one side, and between the bureaucracy and 'subject matter' committees of Congress on the other.

9
The Bureaucracy

The functions of the federal government have so grown that there are few aspects of national life outside the span of its interest, if not its regulation. This growth is reflected in the multiplication of agencies to the point that few people, if indeed any, can really comprehend them in all their ramifications. In picturing this vast bureaucracy, it is, therefore, necessary at the outset to indicate that the description will inevitably be greatly simplified and only a few of the exceptions noted.

Until about 1900, substantive changes in this bureaucracy were almost entirely associated with the growth of and additions to the great departments of Cabinet rank. State, War, and Treasury were the first to appear, but they were soon followed by Navy, Justice, and Post Office. Later to develop were Interior and Agriculture. Comparatively modern are Commerce, Labor, and Air Force – the last accompanied by the grouping of the three branches of the armed services into the single super-Department of Defense. The Department of Health, Education, and Welfare was established in 1953. This was followed by the Departments of Housing and Urban Development, and Transportation. These were both formed by the fusion of previously independent agencies with certain bureaus from existing departments. Most recent achievers of departmental status are Education and Energy; Education's foundation resulted in renaming Health, Education, and Welfare the Department of Health and Human Services. Efforts have been made to give separate departmental status to other federal activities such as public works, health, science; but as yet they have been unsuccessful. Usually the creation of a department was preceded by bureaus or agencies of some sort in its general area, not necessarily specifically attached to one of the existing departments. In other instances, notably Labor, the creation was brought about by sub-dividing a previously existing department. Certain of the departments are themselves 'holding companies' of several subdepartments grouped together for convenience but having little, if anything, more in common than they share with certain bureaus in other departments. For example, the Department of the Interior deals with Indian affairs, territories and insular possessions, fisheries, wildlife, land management, national parks and recreation, reclamation, mining, and other functions. Each of these is incorporated in a separate bureau. There are about twenty-five in all.

The growth of bureaus has, in fact, been more or less continuous from the beginning. However, it is only in the last thirty years or so that agencies not formally designated as departments have, in several instances, themselves reached or exceeded the magnitude of many of the departments. Today, there are a number of such agencies, virtually indistinguishable except in title from the regular departments. The heads of some of them now sit in the Cabinet by invitation of the President. Of these, the National Aeronautics and Space Administration, the National Science Foundation, the Veterans Administration, and the Environmental Protection Agency are perhaps the best known, but there are more than a score of others, the heads of which report directly to the President. It is no accident that many of these are derivatives of the 'science explosion'.

Still another type of agency is the so-called independent commission. These arose along with the growth of government regulation. Typically, they are given regulatory powers over some sector of the economy – rail and truck transport, trade practices, communications, aviation, elections. In this respect, their jurisdiction does not, in fact, differ from many of the powers assigned to the departments or other agencies. Proposals are made from time to time to merge the commissions with existing or new departments. The commission membership ranges from three to eleven. Commissioners are appointed by the President with the approval of the Senate. Many commissions are bipartisan by statute. Appointments are for a stated number of years, and the power of the President to remove a commissioner during his term is usually limited. This is in accord with the usual intent of Congress in setting them up. It was hoped that they would function with a high degree of specialized competence and independence, free from partisan and Presidential pressure. In considerable measure, this hope has been realized. The most serious criticism of these commissions is that they have become clientele-oriented. In other words, they have tended to overlook the broad public interest, in more and more identifying themselves with the areas they had been set up to regulate. The President's authority has been shadowy at best. This has, at times, created serious problems of coordination within the government as a whole. Especially has this been true when a commission's administrative functions overshadowed its judicial functions, as is increasingly the case. There is a tendency to give a commission's chairman certain special administrative powers – a further witness to the changing nature of commission responsibility.

Finally, there has grown up in America, as in England, the 'government corporation'. In America also, it has found considerable favor because a degree of freedom and flexibility is inherent in this administrative device that is not open to the more orthodox type of agency. Usually, but not always, the corporation is created to undertake some specific project or to conduct some business undertaking. The Tennessee Valley Authority and the United States Postal Service are the best known of these, but the whole field of government lending has a number of such corporations, some attached to other departments and agencies.

Without attempting a complete list of these various departments, agencies, commissions, and corporations, it may be useful to indicate the principal ones and note their chief functions if their titles are not sufficiently descriptive.

I. Departments

1 State: foreign affairs and policy; cultural exchange; international, technical, and economic aid.
2 Treasury: internal revenue; customs; custody of funds; currency; debt; internal finance; secret service.
3 Defense: Chiefs of Staff; weapons evaluation; coordination of procurement; research and development; munitions; manpower; military assistance; security; civil defense.

(a) Army: Army; civil works, including harbor installations, flood control, inland navigation; Panama Canal.

(b) Navy: Navy; Marine Corps.

(c) Air Force: Air Force; missiles.

4   Justice: prosecutions, including antitrust and civil rights; Federal Bureau of Investigation; immigration and naturalization; prisons; alien property.

5   Interior: territories; Indian affairs; water and power resources; fisheries and wildlife; national parks; public lands; oil and mineral resources; mapping.

6   Agriculture: promotion and regulation of agriculture; marketing; soil conservation; farm credit; crop insurance; rural electrification; forests; home economics.

7   Commerce: census; statistical services; maritime; promotion of trade and travel; national production; weather bureau; regional commissions; patents; standards; area redevelopment.

8   Labor: employment exchanges; labor standards; employees' compensation; labor statistics; women's affairs; employment security and training; occupational safety and health.

9   Health and Human Services: social security; food and drugs; health services and research; civil rights; aging; disease control.

10 Housing and Urban Development: underwriting housing loans; public housing; model cities; new towns; urban renewal.

11 Transportation: railways; mass transit; highways; airlines; Coast Guard; St Lawrence Seaway.

12 Energy: different types; safety; planning and research; conservation; regulation.

13 Education: grants-in-aid to states and localities; various types and levels; research.

II. Agencies

Action: Peace Corps; Voluntary Citizen Participation.

Environmental Protection Agency.

US Information Agency: Voice of America; overseas libraries; bi-national cultural affairs.

Federal Reserve System (Board of Governors): banking; credit; economic stabilization (partial responsibility).

National Labor Relations Board.

Railroad Retirement Board.

Veterans Administration.

National Mediation Board (for the railroads).

Federal Mediation and Conciliation Service.

National Science Foundation.

General Services Administration: public buildings; archives; supply and procurement.

Selective Service System.

Smithsonian Institution: museums; art galleries; zoo.

National Aeronautics and Space Administration.

Farm Credit Administration.

Small Business Administration.

Federal Council on the Aging.

Federal Emergency Management Agency: prepares for emergencies; aids disaster areas.

Arms Control and Disarmament Agency.

International Development Cooperation Agency: foreign aid; overseas private investment.

Office of Personnel Management: recruiting; classification; Senior Executive Service; management development; labor relations (in the government); salary scales.

Federal Home Loan Bank Board.

Government Printing Office (part of the legislative establishment).

General Accounting Office (part of the legislative establishment).

Library of Congress (part of the legislative establishment); national library; copyright; Congressional research.

Botanic Garden (part of the legislative establishment, administered by the Architect of the Capitol).

III. Independent Commissions (regulatory)

Merit System Protection Board.

Nuclear Regulatory Commission.

Interstate Commerce Commission: railways; motor transport.

Securities and Exchange Commission.

Federal Maritime Commission.

Federal Trade Commission: trade practices.

Federal Communications Commission.

International Trade Commission: promotion; identification of foreign subsidized exports.

Commodity Futures Trading Commission.

Commission on Civil Rights.

Equal Employment Opportunity Commission.

IV. Corporations

Tennessee Valley Authority.

Federal Deposit Insurance Corporation.

Federal Crop Insurance Corporation (attached to Department of Agriculture).

Export-Import Bank.

Pension Benefit Guaranty Corporation.

Panama Canal Commission.

United States Postal Service.

St Lawrence Seaway Development Corporation.

The modern science of administrative management has brought a measure of uniformity into the pattern of organization of each of these units.

Each usually has a political head – political in the sense that the appointment is by the President and subject to Senate confirmation. Usually, but not always, such a head is partisan, in the sense that he is a member of the President's party and in general accord with the President's policies. This is increasingly true also of the chairmen of the independent commissions, where such chairmen have unusual powers. Such political appointments usually also include the under and assistant secretaries or administrators and some of the bureau chiefs. Many of the latter, however, are career men, who are appointed and retain their posts without reference to partisanship. The political head is naturally responsible for his department or agency, but if he is wise, he will confine his own activities largely to the policy and public-relations levels. Thus, he will usually have one or more 'operating men' closely associated with him, perhaps as under or assistant secretaries. Around him will also be grouped certain staff services, usually including a budget officer, a director of personnel, a planning unit, a legal division, a public-relations officer, an office of Congressional liaison, and a reporting unit. Then will come a series of bureaus, each headed by a chief, which perform the actual functions of the unit. These, in turn, will usually be subdivided. Nomenclature at this point becomes even more confused than at the bureau level.

Most departments and agencies and even bureaus have extensive field services. In some instances, these are organized on a state-by-state basis; in others, regions of administrative convenience are established. Some appreciation of the nature and magnitude of the field service is gained through a realization that fewer than 10 per cent of the federal civilian employees, in fact, work in the Washington area. Decentralization creates problems of control at the same time that it offers opportunities for differentiation and local cooperation.

For many years attempts at field level cooperation took the form of regional inter-departmental committees. Two complementary trends have recently occurred so as to make such cooperation more effective. A strong move has set in to make the regions of the various agencies uniform, and to concentrate their regional headquarters in the same city. Some Regional Councils have been established.

Administration is a process of decision-making. This has several entirely natural by-products, yet ones that, as a whole, make government something of a mystery. This decision-making is far from merely a matter of an individual head of a unit deciding something subject to approval by the next man higher up in the hierarchy. American government, like its British counterpart, is filled with procedures designed to assure comment by interested parties prior to decisions – parties not only within or outside the immediate agency, but often altogether outside government. Routing for comment, hearings, advisory committees, and interagency committees are types of devices that mark modern administration in what has been called the 'negotiating society'. No one really knows how many interagency committees are at present operating in the American Government. A recent survey, by no means exhaustive, uncovered nearly 400. A few of these had a statutory base; far more were set up by executive order; many of them grew quite spontaneously from the felt needs of the situation. In the equally important area of contacts with interested outside parties, there is the same gamut from formalization by law to informal representation by interests concerned. Those who feel that lobbying by special interests is largely confined to Congress are quite unaware that the shift in the nature of government from making laws toward continuous intervention in national life has brought in its train a multiplication of the efforts whereby the points of view of interested parties are brought to bear upon appropriate agencies. For example, the International Trade Commission is specifically charged with the responsibility of listening to complaints of those affected by excessive imports.

Finally, it should be noted that, in increasing measure, agencies are allowed to contract with other agencies within and outside the government to perform certain of their functions. The most spectacular use of this power has been by the defense agencies, in a multitude of research contracts. The ramifications of government would appear to reach everywhere. The use of outside consultants has grown. This growth has come to be the subject of considerable criticism.

The personnel of the American federal government reveal both differences and similarities compared with British personnel. Political patronage in America still plays a much greater part in appointments, but the difference is much less than in earlier times. It is difficult to say just how many posts in the United States are still subject to party influence in appointment. In the permanent agencies, the Department of Justice is almost certainly the chief offender. Recent decades have, however, seen periods in which the growth of emergency agencies has been a striking characteristic of the government. The first group of these emergency agencies was to combat the depression; the next group came in with World War II; and still others have been associated with the dramatic postwar events. The very emergency character of these agencies undoubtedly created and still creates a situation whereby members of Congress or influential members of the dominant party organization can usually obtain posts of some sort for moderately qualified persons in whom they might be really interested, without having those persons subjected to the usual competitive screening. A far larger number of those appointed, including many of those going through the normal competition, present letters of recommendation or endorsement from Congressmen or party officials. These letters are very easily obtained and may or may not be a factor in the selection.

It is the American theory, as it is the British, that policy-making positions should be filled by the party in power. In Britain, these are regarded as very few in number, and those selected for them are almost always Members of Parliament. The number of such positions in the United States is considerably greater, including as it does a number of those closely associated with each agency head – many bureau chiefs, most assistant secretaries, a number of advisers and assistants in the departmental or agency headquarters, and most members of the 'independent commissions'. Even in this group of policy-makers career appointments are made with increasing frequency, as are appointments of eminently qualified men (not associated with party) from outside the government. The appointments of Edward Levi as Attorney General, of George Shultz in various capacities, of Robert McNamara as Secretary of Defense, and of Russell Train as head of the Environmental Protection Agency are examples. Where the British and the American systems really differ, to the undoubted detriment of the latter, is in the extent to which the latter still makes available to state and local party organizations large numbers of appointments of federal attorneys, federal judges, and local administrators of emergency agencies. Until recently, collectors of internal revenue were also included in this group. It is not that certain qualifications are not centrally imposed before a party recommendation is accepted, for they usually are. It is rather that, by and large, these appointments represent the principal remains of a patronage system that was, for many decades, characteristic of a far larger section of the federal administration. Over the years, one group after another has been 'bracketed in' – that is, added to the so-called classified service appointed on a merit basis, until only a few groups remain as witness to the old order.

The term 'classified service' is used to cover those employees subject by law to the standard federal practices of appointment by merit; classification according to work performed; and tenure, leave, and retirement provisions. In all, about 1,400,000 are so included. In addition to those in this category, certain groups of employees, notably the Foreign Service of the State Department, are under special merit systems of their own. However, the present very large difference between the number in the classified service and the total number of civilian employees is accounted for by the large number of non-permanent employees in the military and emergency agencies and by the numbers of unskilled laborers who are outside the group. Most of the first group are appointed competitively on a merit basis but without permanent tenure.

At least until the Watergate scandals and the 'anti-bureaucracy' tone of President Reagan's election campaign and subsequent pronouncements, government service as a career had grown greatly in prestige during recent years, though it had not yet achieved the status accorded to it in Britain. Between Watergate and Reagan, Presidents Ford and Carter did much to restore this prestige.

Appointment is usually by competition. This competition usually consists, in the higher ranges, almost entirely of appraisals of previous record plus an interview. Though being re-studied under Reagan, a marked recent trend has been the effort, largely successful, to attract and retain in the service numbers of the finest university graduates. The experience of Britain in recruiting and retaining its 'administrative class' has been one of the major factors in promoting this development. Appointment, even at this level, is usually (though no longer always) more highly specialized than in Britain, the required examinations laying more stress upon the content of the agency's work – economics, agriculture, engineering, forestry, international relations, etc. Another significant difference between the two nations is the extent to which the upper positions in the United States are filled from outside the government. The great growth of government is partly responsible, a growth that found the numbers of executives or specialists qualified for promotion from within the government far too small. However, another and equally important factor lies in the American tendency not to regard a present post or even a present type of occupation as necessarily permanent. Ambition and restlessness both play their part in this attitude. So also does the relatively greater prestige attached to a business career in the United States than in Britain. Men move back and forth between business and government as personal advantage or the call of duty may dictate. So also in increasing measure do the members of university faculties – a development stimulated by, but by no means confined to, the depleting effect of war and the draft and a declining birth rate upon the student rosters. Moreover, those entering the federal employment at the clerical or other very modest levels often tend to continue their education in the evenings in the hope of bettering their status. In Washington, for example, there are at any one time probably some 25,000 or more federal employees studying part-time at the university level. Almost all federal agencies offer in-service training programs.

Salaries, when tenure, leave, and retirement benefits are taken into account, are not unattractive. Clerical salaries are above the average of those in private employment. Professional salaries compare favorably with those of the faculties of the universities. The entering professional salary is about $13,369 per year, but large numbers commence their government careers at higher levels. Non-administrative professional salaries reach their peak at $61,275. For lawyers and physicians, this is rather too low to hold many of the best. Executive salaries compare not too favorably with those in private industry. Their effective peak, with tenure, is $61,275. Most of the newly formed 'Senior Executive Service' may look forward to a peak of $68,200, but tenure is not guaranteed. Bonusses in salary of the SES (except for cost of living increments) must be documented on a merit basis. Cabinet officers receive $66,000. In the rush for adjournment in December 1982, adjustment in the salaries of Cabinet officers was not included. Sometime in the 1983 Congress these will doubtless be adjusted upward. Increments, as distinct from promotions, are standardized. Promotions from one agency to another are fairly frequent. There is regrettably little interchange of personnel with state governments and even less with local governments. Yet, all in all, the American government has made very great strides in the direction of an enlightened and dynamic career service, especially during the past few decades.

Removals are difficult, too difficult, perhaps – not because of legal obstacles, but because of the pressures, political and otherwise, that are usually invoked to prevent them. The recent establishment of the Merit System Protection Board reduces the number of appeals to one or two, and should make severance for cause more easy.

What of the tone of the federal public service? It is difficult to generalize. Recent revelations of corruption have been almost entirely among patronage and temporary employees, except for the General Services Administration. The revelations have been greeted with shock, rather than cynicism. Some of the traditional shortcomings of bureaucracy are conspicuously evident in certain quarters. 'Parkinson's

Law' (the improvisation of 'busy work' to keep everyone fully occupied) and the 'Peter Principle' whereby people are eventually promoted
to their own level of mediocrity, are all too frequent. So also is the fear
of 'making waves' by internal criticism of existing, outmoded practices.
Turnover is very great at the upper levels. Yet considering the magnitude of the tasks entrusted to government, the general impression
gained is one of competence and devotion to duty, liberally inter-
spersed with sufficient instances of brilliance to inspire hope that the
very considerable progress of recent years will be continued. Provision,
by British standards, often seems lavish and even wasteful, yet there
are many examples of the adaptation of scientific management and of
rapid and skilled action that mark American enterprise at its best.

The nature of administration is too little understood. Much of it is,
of course, the direct rendering of aid to persons, groups, and organizations. Some agencies, notably the military, have specific tasks, peculiar
to themselves – tasks of action or preparation for action. Under various
legal rituals, much governmental activity is regulatory. Yet underlying
most peacetime activities and many war-emergency activities are three
factors worth singling out for special mention.

The first of these is the extent to which the bureaucracy has come to
be characterized by the agency-clientele relationship. We have already
called attention, in our discussion of pressure groups and Congress, to
the extent to which the modern society and the modern economy have
come to be dispersive. We have traced this to the specialization of
function characterizing industrial and agricultural production and the
service trades and professions. We have suggested that pressures from
these several groups form the most potent factors in politics, now that
it is understood how tremendously important government intervention
can be in the economic struggle. Resultant legislation more and more
has taken the form of declaration of an objective on behalf of one or
more of these groups, along with the designation or establishment of an
agency in the bureaucracy charged with the continuous task of pursuing
this objective. It is this that has chiefly created the multiplicity of
agencies in the American bureaucracy; it is this that, in major fashion,
has given each its clientele. With organized labor and agriculture, this
process has resulted in an entire department so constituted, but there
are a hundred other examples. Sometimes the agency is arbiter between

rival clienteles, and this inspires units such as the Securities and Exchange Commission or the Federal Reserve. By and large, therefore, the bureaucracy is a not unfaithful mirror of a dispersive society, but considerably modified by the assumptions and symbols and rituals of the public interest under which it operates.[1]

The second basic factor to be noted is that, in a certain sense, the bureaucracy has risen to the status of a fourth branch of government. So close are most of its activities to its various clienteles, so sensitive is it thereby to public opinion that it is often fully as much autonomous as either the executive or Congress, which ostensibly control it. Yet here, too, checks and balances are operative, and it fully shares a mutually interacting role with each.[2]

The third underlying factor to be noticed is the tremendously vital role now played by research throughout almost all the agencies. Government has not only become specialized; it has become technical and professional and computerized, and this demands a research undergirding. Moreover, this research often has purposes and functions that extend far beyond the program of the agency itself. The cost-of-living indexes of the Bureau of Labor Statistics, the business indexes of the Department of Commerce and Federal Reserve Board, the crop forecasts of the Department of Agriculture, to mention but a few, have a prestige and usefulness that match the high competence of the government economists who have devised them, supervised their computation, and interpreted their significance. It was essentially the growth of governmental research in the executive branch that for a time threatened the equilibrium between executive and Congress, through its establishment of a near monopoly of technical competence. Only by meeting this threat in kind has the balance been somewhat restored.

Reorganizations or changes in the structure of the executive branch in America have, until recently, required Congressional sanction, whereas in Britain, for the most part, such changes have been in the sphere of the royal prerogative, to be exercised through the responsible Ministry. The Reorganization Act of 1949 introduced a major improvement in this regard, adding considerably to the adaptability of the federal structure.[3] This was preceded by the survey of this structure and much of its operations by the famous first Hoover

Commission (the Commission on the Organization of the Executive Branch), made up of nominees from and by both the executive and Congress.[4] The Heineman Task Force (Presidential Task Force on Government Organization) and the Ash Council (President's Advisory Council on Executive Organization) were the most recent examples of such advisory bodies.

Under the Reorganization Act and its successors, the President drafts and submits to Congress plans for reorganization of agencies and regrouping of functions as he may see fit. Congress has sixty days in which to consider these plans. Unless one house, by a simple majority, declares its opposition, the plan comes into operation. There is still much to be done. At least one hundred plans have been submitted. About 70 per cent have been put into operation. This Act is temporarily in abeyance, and (1982) President Reagan has not yet asked for its re-enactment. Abolition or addition of departments requires direct action by Congress.

This, in the barest outline, is the American bureaucracy. It represents a force, or forces, of almost incalculable power – political, economic, technical – for good or evil. By all odds, it could be the greatest single force in America today – if it operated with unity of purpose, which it does not. The federal government is by far the largest employer, the biggest spender of money, the greatest wielder of formal power, one of the most influential political lobbies for its own interests. So great and so powerful is it that the question is inevitable: 'Can it be controlled?' We turn next to the American answer to this question.

10

The Control of the Executive

The theory of British governance is clear in that it falls to Parliament to control the executive. Ministers are held responsible. General policy is called into question, especially in the debates on the Queen's speech and the estimates. Details are brought to public attention primarily through the medium of the question time. On certain major matters, if Parliament feels it needs help outside its own membership and the bureaucracy, devices such as the Royal Commission and departmental committee are called into play. There is a generally effective understanding that civil-service personnel themselves shall be shielded from both publicity and criticism. There is also a comfortable feeling that the internal control through the Treasury is reasonably adequate in matters such as economy.

To those accustomed to such a tidy pattern, the sprawl and raucousness of many of the devices by which the American Congress seeks to perform similar functions may easily give a false impression. What reaches the public eye is so often either the spectacular or the trivial that the underlying logic of it all may well be missed.

The word 'control' is popularly used so loosely that it is important to understand at the outset what is really meant. As was suggested in the previous chapter, we face in the bureaucracy the emergence of a force of tremendous potential power – a force which, if it operates within legally prescribed limits and according to popular intent as reflected in the policies of elected officials and other media, can be an instrument of far-reaching effectiveness for the public interest. Conversely, it can become a Frankenstein's monster, a law unto itself, interested largely in its own perpetuation and expansion. Many view the transformation of the original revolutionary zeal of Soviet Communism into the present police state as being of this character. Then, too, there is the vitally important question of bureaucratic honesty and integrity. Controls internal and external can do much to assure that this tremendous machine does not fall into the hands of the unscrupulous, though the final verdict in these matters rests rather with the spiritual forces that so largely determine the mores of a people. In the popular mind, the problem of control involves efficient operation – that is, economy, effectiveness in performance of the several functions, coordination in the bureaucracy as a whole. With its growth in numbers, with the advent of so much that is discretionary in officialdom and so much that can vitally affect the individuals and groups with which officialdom deals, the bureaucracy has come to have very great political power of its own. All too frequently, this is capable of influencing the very electoral process on which its control so largely depends. Finally, much of policy determination itself is inherent in administration. For example, there is the power in foreign relations and in direction of the armed services to create major *faits accomplis*. Another example is the weight of authority that experience with problems gives to a government agency administering a field such as agriculture when it proposes new legislation. Thus, it becomes all too obvious that general policy, as well as detail, is a sphere in which the issue of control of the bureaucracy is vital. All these elements – legality, intent, honesty, integrity, efficiency, political power, policy – are parts or aspects of the problem of control. And we now turn to the consideration of each.

At the outset, it should be noted that in the control of most of these factors, responsibility is shared by the Presidency and Congress. The courts and the General Accounting Office also play limited roles, though the very existence of an overriding judicial control is of vital significance. The General Accounting Office has increasingly been used as an arm of Congress. In the past it was virtually an independent, though not an irresponsible, instrument. Having already discussed the role of the Presidency in these matters, we shall content ourselves at this point largely with underscoring the comment we made previously, to the effect that the Presidency – notably the Office of Management and Budget – is in reality more a partner of Congress in the exercise of control than it is itself the object of such control. The President, as well as Congress, is an elected representative of the people.

One may assume that in general each agency intends to act within the law, though it may at times see how far the law can be stretched. Some agencies have left certain laws unenforced, but have subsequently responded to class action and other law suits which have called for such enforcement. Legality of expenditure is ultimately the province of the General Accounting Office, and its post audit seems thorough enough. Legality of action or inaction may be tested in the courts. Unlike their British counterparts, American public officials must reckon with the higher legal consideration of constitutionality as well as with the ordinary question of whether a given act is *ultra vires* under statute or common law. Appeals from the decisions of administrative tribunals have been numerous. The judicial decisions emerging have been increasingly friendly to administrative discretion in substantive content, but zealous in the emphasis laid upon correct and reasonable procedure. In the further realm of constitutional law, there undoubtedly lies a higher important reserve safeguard against arbitrary extension of a doctrine such as that of inherent executive power. Decisions involving Nixon and his administration point in this direction. There is no historical parallel to Watergate, especially to that aspect of it in which clearly the President himself was involved in the illegal 'cover up' at an early stage; consistently lying to the public about it. Under this extreme test of the American system, the system worked. The President resigned to avoid virtually certain impeachment. He had previously withdrawn what appeared to be potentially a defiance of the Supreme Court. President Ford then pardoned him, it is true; and this pardon remains controversial, not as to Ford's motives, but as to his judgment.

The attempt to impeach President Andrew Johnson was largely political. President Jackson did defy the federal courts and repudiated the treaty with the Cherokee Nation. But this move regrettably had popular support based on the white man's greed.

The control against deliberate distortion of legislative intent is a province that Congress regards as peculiarly its own. Apart from amendment of the law which is not likely to be too practicable a remedy because of the probability of a Presidential veto, the chief weapons of Congress in this field are publicity and the power of appropriation.

Further weapons used by Congress are to fix in a new law its date of termination unless re-enacted, and the frequently used (but judicially untested) power of 'legislative veto of specific regulations issued by an agency'. Theoretically, there should be no problem if laws are carefully drawn, but they are not always so drawn. Then, too, many laws are purposely drawn in general terms so as to allow a very considerable measure of administrative discretion. Laws whose chief content is the declaration of objectives and the creation of instruments to carry them out lend themselves readily to subsequent administrative modification of these objectives. The administration of certain laws may be entirely correct in terms of legality, while at the same time, administration can be in such a fashion as to incorporate the philosophy of the administrator rather than that of Congress. Moreover, Congress may never have made its intention clear in the first place. Price controls can be administered to limit profits more than – or less than – wages. Public power development can be administered to favor public over private distribution thereof in the absence of any law on the subject. With so many laws actually matured in the bureaucracy, the Congress can never be quite certain what 'sleepers', or hidden powers and meanings, may be concealed within the text. In Britain, what seems to be a relative absence of such problems is probably accounted for by two circumstances: the general loyalty of the civil servant to the intent of the minister and the desire to save him embarrassment; and the assumption on the part of the government of public responsibility for all the consequences of a given law, even though it may not have realized them at the time of passage. Separation of the executive from the legislature under the American system normally lessens the former's loyalty to the legislative branch, while at the same time it gives greater subsequent assurance that such deviation from understood intent will be ruthlessly exposed in floor debate and committee investigations. Retribution for noncompliance in America will be exacted most probably through cuts or directives in appropriations. A word of caution should be added at this point against crediting as true all accusations in Congress as to distorted intent. It is common practice for individual members or groups, unable to secure the general support of their colleagues, to charge such distortion on points that were perhaps not even foreseen, let alone specifically passed upon, at time of enactment. It is also the standard tactic of the minority to try to pin the badges of illegality, unconstitutionality, and irresponsibility upon the party in power. These may or may not be true, especially to the extent alleged. None the less, the nature of government today is such that a large measure of discretion must inevitably fall to the bureaucracy; it is surely of importance that the way be open and used to prevent this discretion from being employed contrary to the intent of the body passing the original law. By a rule of the House each committee is directed to exercise 'oversight' over agencies concerned with functions and/or laws falling within that committee's responsibilities. Most committees have established an 'oversight subcommittee' to carry out this function.

It is a sad commentary on the quality of American administration that controls over honesty and integrity must loom as large as they do, not so much with the career civil servant, as with the political appointees. The reason for the very considerable contrast with the British Civil Service has never been satisfactorily explained. The heterogeneity of America, with its consequent relative absence of a universally agreed-upon code of ethics, certainly is a contributing factor. Then, too, American business has enjoyed perhaps the highest prestige of any group in national life, but the heritage of its attitudes of frequently unscrupulous conduct in the not too distant past is still very much with the people. In Britain, other groups – the landed gentry, for example – occupied the center of respect, and integrity and devotion to the public service had come to be closely associated with these groups. America is obviously dealing with the simultaneous presence in its public service of at least three distinguishable standards in ethical codes.

First, there is the standard of the 'politician', in the bad sense of the term – the product of city machines such as the Pendergast Democratic machine of Kansas City or the Philadelphia Republican organization a few decades ago, or of the personal politics associated with many of the county courthouses. 'To the victor belong the spoils' – spoils of office, of contracts, of immunities. Campaigns cost money, and how can money be raised except in return for favors? Out of attitudes such as these, men of warm human friendliness and essential personal integrity – such as the late Al Smith or former President Truman – can arise. But also out of such a milieu can come those whose conscience is blunted and whose motives are self-seeking. To the extent that federal patronage still is associated with party organizations, we must expect a considerable amount of dereliction – not among career men, but among political appointees.

The second standard is made up of attitudes transferred from private business. This is competitive; this is profit-seeking. It has, on the other hand, now largely purged itself of dishonesty and has received a considerable transfusion of the attitude of social responsibility. Nevertheless, government is mixing in business in a large way. Business, labor, and other groups seek to place in office their friends, whose earlier and lesser loyalties then, far too frequently, bring betrayal of the larger public interest in matters such as the letting of contracts or the making of wage settlements. The line between the normal wholesome functioning of the democratic process and compromises with integrity is extremely fuzzy at this point. Another fuzzy point is the frequency with which government officials are subsequently employed by businesses with which they have had dealings.

The third standard is, of course, that of public service. Integrity, a much more inclusive term than honesty, is an attribute of this standard.

How then to secure honesty and an increasing measure of integrity that will give people merited confidence in their government? This question is a very perplexing one to Americans today. Crude peculation is likely to be uncovered by the ordinary internal accounting controls. It is not a serious problem. Scandals in the Bureau of Internal Revenue, where tax favors were extended for personal considerations, represented a more difficult type to detect. An alert Congress has been invaluable in this regard, and Senators Kefauver and Williams became national heroes for their role in investigations. Another approach has been urged by men like Senator Douglas and Representative Bennett, resulting in the formulation by Congress of a code of ethics for public officials. This code goes beyond the law and may serve as a crystallized norm for all public officials to replace the confusion we have already mentioned. Recently, Congress has authorized the appointment of an 'inspector general' for each major unit of government. He is given by law a measure of independence from the head of the agency to investigate alleged violations of law, conflict of interest, gross inefficiency, or ethical deviations.

The weapon of Congressional investigation is essential. Leaving such matters wholly to the executive invites the temptation to cover up, lest exposure should weaken its prestige. On the other hand, the American electorate rightly honors its crusaders. Congressional investigations not only have their own special staffs, they also have a considerable measure of concrete assistance in obtaining information from inside the executive and from members of the public. Such investigations are peculiarly adapted to those situations in which no law has been violated, but in which there has been an apparent betrayal of public trust. By focusing on ethics rather than legality, they can perform the highly important function of crystallizing opinion as to what things are or are not to be done. This is not to say that all investigations are noble in motive or nobly conducted. Many fall far short of such standards. Yet Madison's point made almost two centuries ago retains much of its original validity: the American system harnesses the self-interest of different institutions to check each other in such a way that perhaps the people so governed are better served than they would be by concentration of power and responsibility.

Efficiency as an objective of control requires more precise definition. Actually, three principal values seem to be involved in this concept. The first is economy in financial terms or, more fundamentally, in the use of men and materials. The second is effectiveness – that is, the performance of functions as entrusted, accurately, expeditiously, and in full measure. The third has to do with coordination – the integration of the several parts and objectives in such a fashion that there is no incompatibility or lost motion. The establishment of priorities in expenditure is akin to this. A few words are in order at this point concerning effectiveness and coordination. Financial concerns, processes, and controls are sufficiently important to merit a separate chapter (see Chapter 12 below).

We have already indicated the roles played respectively by the Office of Management and Budget and the Appropriations Committees of Congress in economy. The former parallels closely the function of Treasury control; the latter have no real parallels in British national government. Perhaps the detailed scrutiny of estimates imposed by the finance committees of certain of the county boroughs comes the nearest to it in British experience. The cuts imposed by Congress, at the behest of the Appropriations Committees, in the estimates that have already been approved by the Office are often fairly substantial although some cynics doubt how far they go beyond what is subsequently included in supplemental appropriations. Some cuts are expected in any event. As regards specific items of extravagance, the Congressional committees are aided from time to time by tips or information from many sources both within and outside the government. Efforts to establish cost figures based on workload have made some progress. The staff work of the committees constitutes another invaluable aid. Yet, when all is said and done, Congress is still largely at the mercy of the departments, especially the Department of Defense because of the sheer magnitude and technical nature of its operations. The necessary secrecy surrounding many military matters constitutes another hazard in this particular instance. *Ex post facto* investigation of expenditures is one of the statutory functions of the Congressional Committees on Government Operations; and these Committees occasionally turn out reports of considerable influence in future estimates. In such investigations all relevant committees of Congress now can receive very great assistance from studies by the General Accounting Office. Once the Office of Management and Budget has adopted departmental estimates, all concerned in the executive branch normally unite in refusal to indicate priorities therein to Congress, defending rather the equal importance of each item. Along with this goes a refusal to disclose to Congress the content of the Bureau's own hearings on the estimates. Thus Congress has to do the best it can. The House seems to be somewhat bolder because it knows that the Senate can put right any cuts that seem likely inadvertently to result in the impairment of an important function of government.

It should be understood that, by and large, the American government seeks to impose economy by the multiplication of hazards to expenditure. First, an agency has its own budget officer who, because he must bear the brunt of justifying the estimates, must first be convinced that specific proposals for expenditure are in line with what is necessary to attain the results proposed. The next hazard is the Office of Management and Budget, usually armed also with certain policy directives of the President as to the total figure to be aimed at. This is followed by the Appropriations Subcommittee of the House of

Representatives, which holds the principal legislative hearing, and then by a not always perfunctory consideration by the Committee as a whole. The entire House next has its turn, and amendments calling for further reductions are of late more frequently successful than those calling for increased expenditure. Similar hazards face the estimates in the Senate, though recent experience indicates that this body is somewhat more likely to restore cuts than to add to them. Finally, either President or Congress may impose further economies during the ensuing year – though supplemental appropriations may likewise be sought and obtained. President Nixon went far beyond any of his predecessors in 'impounding' appropriated funds. This refusal to spend was partly an economy measure, partly the result of evaluation of certain functions which indicated that they were not in fact attaining their objectives. Congress subsequently retaliated by passing an act severely restricting a President in this regard. The President also lost a number of court cases in which he (the Executive) was forced to make such expenditure. What is the net result of legislative scrutiny? In the field of public works, proposed expenditure tends to be postponed or slowed down rather than ultimately reduced. In other fields, material cuts are made by Congress – usually, but not always, from the *increases requested* rather than from the previous year's figure. A very large part of the estimated expenditure is contractual in nature and not subject to cutting of this sort – interest on the debt, subsidies to the states that rest upon a legislative formula, veterans' benefits, pensions. All are substantial money users, and on all of these, the Appropriations Committees are virtually powerless unless the legislative requirements are themselves changed. Some items are increased. More and more, both branches of government are forced to consider *priorities*.

The effectiveness of administration is a subject of constant Congressional concern. The committee hearing and investigation are the real American parallel to the question time in the House of Commons. In addition, discussion on the floor of both houses of Congress can and does direct attention to inefficiency in operations, even though, unlike the House of Commons, there is no representative of the agency criticized present. Most agencies can find spokesmen among the Congressmen themselves, who are willing to reply at a later session, even if they are not ready on the spot. The press release or public statement of the agency head – or even of the President – is also available. Much of this criticism is informal, by telephone or otherwise; and the matter is settled 'out of court'. It should be borne in mind at this point that the American people look to their representatives in Congress – far more than British constituents do to Members of Parliament – for redress of grievances. They send Congressmen suggestions for improved public service, and they also write to the President on matters of this sort. By and large, the agencies are extremely sensitive to criticism, even by a single member of Congress. Thus, through various channels, a continuous barrage of reactions from those affected by, or those noticing, ineffective or faulty operations goes on. Conversely, there are instances of praise and gratitude as well.

Sometimes criticism reaches the stature of a full-fledged investigation. The investigation may be held by the Standing Committee charged with responsibility for the field, or by one of the Committees on Government, or it may be by a special Committee created for the purpose. The investigation is an exceedingly flexible weapon of control. It can range widely; it can focus narrowly. It can be very simple – the result of a mere request on the part of a committee for explanation of certain matters, usually, but not always, resulting in the attendance of someone from the agency at a public hearing. On the other hand, as was the case with the Watergate and campaign practices investigation by the Senate Committee chaired by Senator Ervin, the hearing may go on for months and pass in review matters of the highest importance. Or the investigation may be continuous – as for example, that by the committee presided over by the then Senator Truman during World War II, which ranged widely over much of the war effort. The Standing Committees of Congress are specifically charged under the Legislative Reorganization Act of 1946 with 'watchfulness' over the corresponding agencies in the bureaucracy. Where the committee or subcommittee is itself composed of members chosen largely from regions whose economic interests coincide with the purpose for which the agency was created, the committee is likely to be especially zealous to see that the work is well performed, but it is also likely to be less ready to criticize policy recommendations. Even more striking are the iron triangles or sub-systems or 'whirlpools' at the subcommittee level. Here the characterization of 'co-conspirators' is not too strong when applied to the subcommittee members, the bureau in the Executive Branch and the relevant lobbyists concerned with a particular governmental activity. To call this 'oversight' is a misuse of the term.

Pressure groups have their spokesmen in Congress. They serve as ready and alert agents to see to it, as far as agitation, criticism, and questions will do the job, that the group's interests are furthered up to the intent of the relevant law, and that these interests are not harmed by a hostile administration without a clear showing of administrative authority. Finally, it should be noted that the influence and activity of the Appropriations Committees extend considerably beyond considerations of economy. In the language of the appropriations bills, in criticism, in informal guidance, or in explicit directives, controls are exercised over administration, organization, and policy which make these Committees potentially the most powerful of the weapons in the Congressional arsenal of control.

On balance, Congress is highly successful in its efforts to keep the administration even more sensitive to public opinion than it otherwise would have been. In its questions and investigations, it goes far beyond what would be regarded as appropriate in Britain. This has undoubtedly discouraged many from entering and remaining in the public service. It has, in many instances, itself been costly of time and effort. The weapon of investigation has at times been irresponsibly exercised. Yet the public interest aroused, the quality of constant alertness created, the sense of accountability generated by Congressional investigations are surely assets of very great value. Over and above this, there exists an impressive record of concrete reforms and results – and, conversely, of vindications of agencies through criticism being pursued to a conclusion. This record makes the general verdict on Congressional investigations unmistakably favorable.

Unfortunately, the record on the type of control that looks toward coordination is less successful. Neither the Presidency nor even the Congress has succeeded in developing institutions as yet really adequate for this colossal task. There is grave doubt as to whether efforts along this line have even kept pace with the growth of government. Contradictory policies continue to be administered in the bureaucracy and generated in Congress. Duplications of activities become notorious and yet linger on for years without remedy. Every so often, there is a real gain – or at least the groundwork is laid for a gain – as, for example, in the grouping of the armed services in the single Department of Defense. Yet the Army Engineers, the Bureau of Reclamation, and the Department of Agriculture continue to generate rival, or at least unintegrated, plans to develop and harness the water resources of the same river valley. Commodity experts cover much the same ground in their research in a half-dozen agencies.

Instruments of coordination exist: in the National Security and the Domestic Councils, in the Office of Management and Budget, and the Council of Economic Advisers; in the bureaucracy, in the form of inter-departmental committees; in Congress, in the Appropriations, Government Operation, Governmental Affairs, and Joint Economic Committees. Yet the individual agencies are powerful and usually resist integration; they also have their powerful defenders in Congress. Again a key factor is the growth in power of the subcommittees.

On the horizon is the question of another aspect of control, the full answer to which is not yet clear. This is the problem of the political power – especially at election time – of the executive branch. It has two principal facets. The first is the sheer number of voters represented by the government service and their families. This electorate's reasonable satisfaction as a group with its own status quo, or fear of change with a new party in power, can give a very great advantage to an existing administration in seeking votes. Legislative efforts have been made to prohibit political activity on the part of the mass of government officials;[1] but this does not and cannot meet the central problem of the vested interests of the group as a whole. The second aspect involves more those at the policy level in the executive. So many powers discretionary as to time and extent are now vested in the executive that these powers can, in a peculiar sense, be all too readily wielded in such fashion as to affect an election. Temporary stimuli may be applied to employment; benefit checks may be mailed out to farmers, veterans, pensioners, and others just before election; credit controls can be eased or local improvements announced at times best suited to influence voters. There probably is, and probably can be, no control over this type of sharp practice, except for education of the public to assure that in some measure, at least, it may be exposed and thus boomerang.

We leave until the next two chapters the questions of the control of public policy and of finance.

In concluding this part of the discussion of control of the bureaucracy, it should be underscored how much more Congress is concerned with administration, even with its details, than is Parliament. Congress constantly passes laws, detailed laws, to which it has given most thorough consideration, governing personnel management in all its major aspects – recruiting, promotions, pay scales, retirement, severance, equal opportunity for minorities, women, and (in certain circumstances) the handicapped and the aging. Likewise, it regulates the purchase and disposal of supplies, the letting of contracts, and many accounting procedures. It insists on the right to initiate, or at least to pass upon, organizational changes. In this regard, certain bureaus especially seem to have commended themselves to Congressional support and protection against change. Congress still dictates or passes upon thousands of appointments, and interests itself in many removals. It decides, in detail, the location of most major, and many minor, public works. Individual members concern themselves with still more specific decisions – veterans' claims, price regulations, issuance of licenses, draft exemptions, prosecutions before regulatory commissions. Much of this individual intervention is to the good, tempering bureaucratic rigidity and showing how measures operate in practice. Much of it is obviously bad. Whether good or bad, it represents a part of the American government in operation, a concept of legislative concern in administration foreign to British views. In considerable measure, it emanates from that localism which, for good or evil, remains an important part of American government. There are few agreed-upon, exclusive spheres under a regime of separation of powers and checks and balances. Loyalty is dual. If control is to include influence, there is fully as much influence, in terms of the effects of bureaucratic pressures on Congress, in one direction as in the other.

II

The Sources of Public Policy

The sources of British public policy are reasonably clear. The crystal-lization of viewpoints in the electorate, the maturing of programs in the bureaucracy, and the ideas of the Cabinet – these are translated into action through Parliament in general and by the responsible ministry in particular. In America, there is a situation of much greater diffusion. We have noted the separate strands from time to time, and the time has come to bring them together.

It may be helpful at the outset to recognize that public policy emerges in three somewhat differentiated types of decision. Most decisions are notable for their continuity with what has gone before; they are an extension of an existing trend. Such decisions are those extending the coverage of social insurance; refining the process of crop control or expansion; bringing an additional industry within the sphere of government regulation. Typically, these arise from further pressures on the part of the group or groups securing the original legislation, or from the experience of the administering agency, or from both. In decisions of the second type, a government occasionally decides either to reverse a previous policy or to enter a new area of activity. These involve sharp breaks with the past. President Reagan has already achieved many such: he looks forward to more. We may also note a third type of decision, not too sharply differentiated, but nevertheless sufficiently so to be singled out for separate analysis. This is the institution of integrating or coordinating elements in two or more earlier policies that experience has proved somewhat contradictory. Of course, the lines between these three types are anything but sharply drawn, and most important decisions contain elements of each. In general, decisions of the first type are relatively easily made in both Britain and the United States, whereas decisions of the second type, the breaks with the past, are much more difficult. The methods by which decisions of this type are made are sharply different in the two countries. Integrating decisions of the third type require the kind of definition and enforcement of over-all goals that so often seem to depend upon a war for their realization.

In the United States, three major forces may be distinguished operating in policy formulation. The first of these – political dispersiveness – has been referred to many times. It reflects the division of the electorate into economic and other groups. In the two major political parties, it shows itself in the national strategy of trying to create coalitions of the maximum percentage of the maximum number of these groups, and trying to assure that at least a minority of each of the major groups is found among the party supporters. Platforms thus tend to contain something for everyone – couched in sufficiently vague terms to antagonize no one. Candidates in the campaigns denounce straw men and praise all groups in generalities. The groups, on their part, try to pin down the candidates to specific commitments. Once the election is over, the battle is transferred to Congress and the executive. We have seen the by-products of this dispersiveness in the membership of many of the standing committees and subcommittees of Congress and in the multiplication of bureaus in the executive with clienteles drawn from the corresponding groups in the electorate. The common interest and origin of a subcommittee and a bureau, together with the presence in Washington of representatives of the special groups, tend to create the phenomenon of 'government by whirlpools'.

I have called attention to this in another book:

One cannot live in Washington for long without being conscious that it has these whirlpools or centers of activity focusing on particular problems. The persons who are thus active – in agriculture, in power, in labor, in foreign trade, and the parts thereof – are variously composed. Some are civil servants, some are active members of the appropriate committees (and subcommittees) in the House and Senate, some are lobbyists, some are unofficial research authorities, connected with the Brookings Institution or with one of the universities, or even entirely private individuals. Perhaps special correspondents of newspapers are included. These people in their various permutations and combinations are continually meeting in each other's offices, at various clubs, lunching together, and participating in legislative hearings or serving on important but obscure committees set up within the department. Among such human beings interested in a common problem, ideas are bound to emerge – ideas for programs, ideas for strategy. . . .

The relationship among these men – legislators, administrators, lobbyists, scholars – who are interested in a common problem is a much more real relationship than the relationship between Congressmen generally or between administrators generally.[1]

Within the governmental structure, this often means that the relationships and rapport between a Congressional committee or subcommittee and a bureau are more real than between the bureau and the Presidency or between the committee and Congress as a whole. In general, this means that legislation that merely or largely involves continuity with an already existing policy is usually adopted without too much difficulty – unless there are strong counterforces in another bureau or another part of Congress. In this fashion, dispersiveness tends to perpetuate itself. Sometimes the initiating factor is the pressure group; sometimes it is the experience of the administering bureau; less often it is within the Congressional committee, an indispensable element whose favorable reaction must be obtained.

A special type of dispersiveness, by all odds the most marked in Congress, is the localism already mentioned. Most frequently, this is merely one manifestation of the economic group activity previously mentioned, underscoring the geographic concentration of certain interests such as silver, cotton, or irrigation – or the demands for protective tariffs or quotas on particular commodities. Its other major aspect focuses attention on the distribution of federal funds for public works or subsidies of one type or another. In the bureaucracy, this localism undoubtedly has some expression in so far as the field services of particular agencies are inevitably influenced by the point of view of the people in whose territory they operate. With Congressmen, regard for localism is usually a matter of political survival, and defeat usually awaits the man who is not zealous in the interest of his district or state. Moreover, Congress today finds itself almost the only guardian of the vitality of state and local government, now that the Supreme Court has let down the barriers to federal action in so many fields. The executive is inherently national in its viewpoint where programs are involved.

The emphasis of President Reagan on making transfers of power back to the states and localities is unique in its prospect of some success, although Nixon predated him in theoretical advocacy.

Along with dispersiveness – political, economic, social, and governmental – another important contributory factor in the type and content of policy is certainly technical specialization. It tends to focus attention less on pressures and more on facts. We have already had several occasions to mention this as a growing and all-pervading accompaniment of modern legislation and administration.

In Congress, unlike Parliament, there is a most marked response to this trend in the use of standing committees and subcommittees to concentrate year after year on particular problem areas. In part because of the seniority practice, there is a fairly high degree of continuity of membership on these committees. Added to these factors are professional staffs and the further availability of specialists from the Congressional Research Service and the General Accounting Office. In this fashion and through the further acquisition of information in committee hearings, Congress has adapted itself to a technical age with considerably less diminution of its genuinely substantive contribution to policy than has been the case in most representative assemblies. Not only has this been important in the detailed scrutiny of proposals for extensions of existing policy of the type already discussed; even more does it lend itself to policy decisions of the second type – those which involve a reversal or break with the past or the entry into a new field. The Taft-Hartley and the Landrum-Griffin Labor Relations Acts, the manpower program and the International Development Association are examples. So also are the Congressional contribution to a changed Viet Nam policy, Congress' acceptance of the bold new orientation toward international cooperation, and the Civil Rights Act of 1964. The occasional establishment of special committees is a further example of the adaptability of Congress in bringing specialized knowledge to bear upon the analysis of a new problem, or a new approach to an old problem. The National Aeronautics and Space Act of 1958 is a good instance of this.[2]

In the Executive Branch, technical specialization is most evident in development of a continuous policy. It is much less often used to generate a new policy, though, notably in the military, research and analysis bodies exist that are specifically charged with the responsibility of challenging old concepts. This is an interesting and courageous attempt to adapt bureaucracy to the occasional need for reorientation. In the Presidency also, the use of special commissions and task forces has similar possibilities. These were heavily utilized by President Johnson in developing his 'Great Society' program.

There is a tremendous body of relevant experience flowing in day by day to the various bureaus. Analysts of a high order are constantly at work interpreting the data and turning their findings over to their political chiefs with recommendations that they be translated into legislative proposals or shifts in administrative directives. Congress normally makes use of this experience through the routing of relevant legislative proposals to the bureaus for comment and through attendance by the bureau representatives as witnesses at committee hearings. Memoranda and evidence are the subject of study not only by the committee members but also by their professional staffs. More and more, all concerned seek to base agreement upon factual information and thorough analysis. This is an increasing factor in the growth of the nonpartisan approach to policy formulation to which we have already called attention.

Measures of the third, or integrating and coordinating, type emerge considerably less rapidly, both in Congress and in the executive. Clashes between rival groups force attention to shortcomings in the dispersive approach. The technically competent analyst – whether legislative or bureaucratic – is bound to take note of less desirable secondary or derivative effects of given proposals. During a war, integrating bodies multiply in the bureaucracy, bodies that inevitably leave some traces in peacetime. Within the Presidency, the Council of Economic Advisers has a brief to watch for this type of problem, as does its counterpart in Congress, the Joint Economic Committee. Except under the impetus of some transcending national emergency, integrating policy has had terrific obstacles to overcome in the shape of groups, committees, and bureaus accustomed to behave in dispersive fashion. Yet this is the very center of the public interest. Proposals to reorganize the Executive Branch usually have this motivation.

The Reagan administration has created a task force to sift through existing regulations generated by departments and agencies, so as to recommend eliminations on the grounds of being unnecessary, unproductive, harmful, conflicting, and costly, especially to business. It already has had considerable effect.

Leadership in policy adoption is widely diffused in the American system. The President undoubtedly performs the greatest single role. The electoral system tends to make him the President of *all* the people and not of a particular economic group or groups. The widespread nature of his support gives him a self-confidence corresponding to his national stature. He cannot be elected or re-elected by the votes of his party alone. There are not enough of them. Always he must command a considerable measure of support from independents, a support that he constantly seeks to increase during his term of office. The mass media of radio, television, and the press are at his command when he wishes to use them. His messages are widely read and strenuously debated. He has the virtually unlimited capacity to focus attention on any subject he may choose. Appeals to party loyalty are still of considerable effect in certain quarters; and he may, and does, seek to mobilize group pressures on behalf of measures he espouses. Patronage and location of public works are minor weapons, possibly effective in marginal instances. The veto power is often threatened to obtain modifications of proposed measures. The President can mobilize facts and arguments almost at will by calling upon the bureaus.

On a smaller scale members of his Cabinet and heads of agencies can and do exercise considerable leadership. Their public-relations offices issue a constant stream of releases and study public reaction and probable trends. They cultivate key members of Congress.

Within Congress, there also develop centers of leadership – sometimes in advance of the executive, sometimes in support, sometimes in opposition. Many members, especially in the Senate, have had political and administrative careers of great distinction. The floors of both houses provide forums that can give men national stature. Committee chairmen have within their own spheres great, though decentralized, opportunities for leadership. During the years 1958–60, the Majority Leader of the Senate assumed the posture of an alternate to the President in formulating a national program. The Democratic majorities in both houses in 1975 struggled to produce alternatives to President Ford's economic and energy programs. So also is the current Democratic majority in the House, led by Speaker O'Neill; and conferences of the party leaders and state governors, regionally and nationally.

It must be borne in mind that much of the leadership in policy in Congress is not of the spectacular kind. Many of the most effective and influential members do their best work in executive sessions of committees and in informal contacts with their fellows. Not infrequently, they find their chief asset is their superior command of facts, whether acquired as firsthand knowledge or by judicious use of staff and support agency aid. A reputation for independence is usually a greater asset than party loyalty in obtaining election to Congress. The constant shifting in the proportions and personnel of Congress in support of or in opposition to measures is itself indicative of a highly fluid situation in which leadership (as against discipline) has an unusual opportunity to operate.

In conclusion, one sees how difficult it is to generalize as to the sources of public policy. Any measure of any real importance probably owes something to all the forces mentioned. Into it have gone the pressures – support, modification, opposition – of the groups of society affected. Into it has gone the personal contribution of the President or of members of his team in the Cabinet. Into it have gone the backgrounds and slants of the members of Congress – especially those of the committees that have worked on it. Into it also has gone the technical competence, the specialized knowledge of the analysts of the bureaus and the Congressional staffs and support agencies.

If a major change is contemplated, unlike the procedure in Britain there must be *general* support for it – and not support from one class or party alone, as, for example, in the case of the nationalization of steel by the Labour Party. Congress by itself can seldom have its way, for the President can veto, and that veto usually reflects the opposition of either the bureaus concerned or some virtually united groups in the electorate; or it stems from a conviction that the measure in question has certain over-all effects harmful to the economy or society as a whole. A veto can be overridden in Congress only by a two-thirds vote of each house, and the election system is such that this ordinarily cannot be attained on a major measure unless at least a substantial fraction of each of the three major groups – business, agriculture, and labor – support it.

Actually, it is probable that each of these three groups incorporates its strongest veto power in a particular institution. The overrepresentation in the Senate of the smaller agricultural states, together with Senators from other states with substantial rural populations, guarantees that no important legislation hostile to agriculture can ever pass. Similar guarantees against punitive legislation for business are found in the House of Representatives, where members from growing suburban districts unite with the conservative representatives of the small towns and villages of the East, Middle West, and South to give this body its usually more conservative economic tinge. On his part, the President, through his power of veto, usually may be counted on to safeguard the position of organized labor, for it is he who is chosen under an electoral system that requires substantial support from the large industrialized states as a condition of success. The cardinal error of the Republicans in nominating Goldwater in 1964 was their failure to take this factor into account. The rise of public interest lobbies is modifying these group biases also.

Nor can a President obtain a major change on his own initiative, unless he can likewise surmount the hazards of Congressional procedure. These hazards are not readily surmounted if any major group or region in the electorate is united in its opposition – even supposing the President wished to do violence to this group, which is unlikely.

If we look at our consideration of the control of the bureaucracy as well as at the sources of public policy, certain attributes of the American system are clear. No important center of power can long exist without first having to convince its constitutional equal that its existence is justified. This is the modern significance of separation of powers – an institutionalizing of the responsibility for carrying conviction on the part of one's equals, prior to acceptance of leadership. It applies to Congress over against the executive; and to the executive over against Congress. Unlike Parliament, there is no party discipline strong enough in Congress to enforce conformity, if conviction is lacking. Moreover, the equality is no longer merely one of constitutional position; with the growth of Congressional staff, it is once again an equality of technical competence as well.

Thus far, the sources of public policy have been considered largely in terms of the institutions of government and their interrelations, and only secondarily in terms of issues. Even in this latter respect, the emphasis has been upon group or regional interests rather than upon ideological cleavages. Yet, in any representative government resting upon popular suffrage, the question ultimately is: 'What are the basic attitudes of the electorate?'

President Reagan's projected record budget deficit for 1984 underscores his (and the public's) realization that the federal government has gone too far and attempted too much. This was enormously complicated by the depression of 1982 – for which the present administration blames the past – and the past, the present. They may both be right.

A favorite approach is to separate persons into 'liberals' and 'conservatives', or into 'innovators' and 'consolidationists'. At this stage, it is probable that none of these terms is very meaningful. Certainly, at one end of the spectrum of public opinion, there are large numbers of people who, on principle, react against the use of government as an instrument, and a fair number of them – the 'radical right' – are deeply emotional on the subject. At the other end of the spectrum, there is a group of about the same size who are predisposed toward use of the government to solve a problem, and a fair number of them go beyond this to the stage of constant advocacy of ever new governmental activity and planning. But between these two groups stand perhaps half or more of the American electorate, people who are ideologically neither conservative nor liberal – but who are *pragmatic*. In other words, if an important problem emerges in national life or international affairs, it is to be faced, accepted, studied, and solutions are to be proposed. Solutions, in turn, are to be studied on their merits, including consideration of their secondary effects – and in all probability, an eventual consensus will be achieved, involving some combination of the government and the private sectors, and, in the governmental sector, participation at the state and local as well as the national level. This is the so-called mainstream of American political behavior and the ultimate source of most policy changes.

12

Finance and Fiscal Policy

A few fundamentals, constitutional, legislative, and organizational, should be summarized at the outset of this all-important chapter.

Proposed laws have sundry origins. They may emerge from Congressional committee deliberations. They may originate in a single member. They may be found in the President's State of the Union and other messages. Lobbyists and other members of the public may suggest or pressure for the introduction of bills.

All laws for setting up agencies or calling for expenditures are alike in authorizing appropriations. They do not by themselves have the power to appropriate. The authorization may take the form of 'such sums as may be necessary' or they may authorize sums 'not to exceed specific amounts', or they may not use the word 'authorize' at all, but may prescribe a certain function or formula which adds to the cost of government.

All appropriations must be in separate bills, which follow a different procedure. Even though an activity may have been authorized, Congress must wait for recommendations of its Appropriations Committee. They may delay or refuse an appropriation, or cut a specifically authorized figure or they may be generous. Because of this, the House Appropriations Committee has been called a 'third House of Congress'. However, as we shall see later, by a program of entitlements, mandated contracts, and other devices, Appropriations Committees have been effectively bypassed in the majority of expenditures.

The landmark dates in the current budget and fiscal policies of the United States were the Budget and Accounting Act of 1924 and the

Budget and Impoundment Act of 1974. The thrust of the 1924 Act was to establish the President as the initial source of the federal budget. This procedure is 'from the top down' and not scattered sources among the committees of Congress as hitherto. Congress serves as a review body.

The established procedure requires that the agencies responsible for particular activities[1] shall first submit their estimates of cost for the fiscal year commencing the following October to the Office of Management and Budget by the first of October of the preceding year.[2] Whatever is agreed upon in the executive branch is then submitted to Congress (usually in late January) as the executive budget.

The primary responsibility for detailed review was (and still is) assigned to the two Appropriations Committees, and by them reassigned to subcommittees responsible for one or more departments and agencies. With these subcommittees rested the responsibility for a 'line by line' study of what the President had asked for. 'Success' was measured by the sum total of savings resulting from such studies. Before each subcommittee appeared the budget officers, agency heads, and unit chiefs of each unit, to answer questions and justify their estimates. With relatively few exceptions, as the budgets grew in complexity, and the nation grew, and the gross national product grew, attention was primarily directed to requests for specific increases. Occasionally one of these subcommittees favoring a particular function would vote a further increase, but for the most part economies were sought. Under the Constitution, the House would take the initiative of introducing the first bills, leaving it basically to the Senate to serve as a further review agency. In both houses, floor amendments might alter committee decisions.

In general, the Congressional strategy was to multiply the hazards to expenditures. Until the liberal Democratic revolution of 1977, members of the Appropriations Committees (especially in the House) were usually chosen from safe districts, and met in executive sessions for their 'mark ups' or final decisions. Thus, the hazards or hurdles were: the agencies must convince the bureau of the budget, and then the President; the agencies must convince the subcommittees and their staffs in the two houses; the reports of the subcommittees must convince the full committees; in the House the committee reports must be routed to its Rules Committee, which might exact a further reduction (or increase) as the price for sending the finished product to the floor, perhaps with a rule limiting floor amendments (a 'closed' rule). Then the bill's committee supporters must face the parent body as a whole, who as often would impose further cuts, as vote increases. Normally a bill would escape relatively unscathed. Many floor challenges were met with the argument that, if the amount appropriated were found to be too low, the need could be met in the Spring or Summer deficiency or supplemental bills, which were in general used to correct under-estimates of receipts or needs.

On taxation and revenue, the House Ways and Means Committee operated on the assumption that additional taxes or other changes were bad, and often unsettling to the business world. This committee also had the responsibility for amendments to the Social Security Act, the public debt, international trade, and revenue sharing. The regime of Wilbur Mills as chairman (before his resignation) had become legend-ary. Again we had committee members from safe seats, largely senior, and hence more conservative. While Mills was chairman, he persuaded his colleagues to have no subcommittees, thus avoiding a spawning of multi-sources of legislation. Pressure groups who wished minor con-cessions would concentrate on the Senate Finance Committee. For years increments of tax receipts in a rising economy would provide funds enough for increasing expenditure without adding to the existing tax rates. This situation occurred again after the great depression.

There took place in the late 1960s and 1970s something of a revolu-tion in public opinion. This reflected itself in a liberal ascendency in Congress and a renewal of the dynamism of the 'welfare state' of Franklin Roosevelt in Lyndon Johnson's 'war on poverty'. This had also been foreshadowed in the expansion of beneficiaries under social security – a trend which continued until the modest proposals for curtailment likely to be agreed upon in 1983.

Structurally a number of changes were made. After Mills left Ways and Means, the Committee was ordered to establish subcommittees. The fiscal committees changed from regimes of closed sessions to predominantly open ones, even in the highly sensitive mark-up stage of a bill. This exposed members to direct pressure from various welfare beneficiary groups, as well as from the business and other special interest groups who were more interested in special tax favors in the form of loopholes for tax exemptions – later to be known as 'tax expenditures'. In all but one of the last 22 years, there were deficits – relatively small at first, but under Reagan and the recession reaching the $100 billion mark, and headed toward $200 billion in fiscal 1984. The total public debt has passed the trillion mark and will approach a trillion and a half by October 1983. Until the Federal Reserve Board imposed tight money restraints, interest rates soared and so did inflation. The recession ultimately helped to bring on a fall in inflation and interest rates.

There were other factors in the budget mess. The House Democratic Caucus as early as 1977 extended its power to vote secretly on committee (and eventually Appropriations subcommittee) chairmanships. They raised their party quota in the House to a 2 to 1 ratio in several important committees. They packed the two fiscal committees with members from their now overriding liberal wing. 'Pork barrel' politics in water projects, federal subsidies in construction, and location of defense-related installations (beyond need) could and did command sufficient bipartisan majorities to override Presidental vetoes.

Curtailment of Presidential power followed the Nixon errors. Before the Budget and Impoundment Act of 1974, Presidents had been able to exercise a kind of limited item veto by not spending certain portions of the appropriated funds. Congress under Title 10 of the Act, retained to itself the power of approving or disapproving these individual 'impoundments'.

But this Act also included a major device for imposing on itself a greater Congressional responsibility over and above the ritualistic hazard of 'considering' increasing a previously set limit to the national debt. It did this by establishing Budget Committees in both houses. However, these belong, not so much in the historical section of this chapter, but in the description of what are the fiscal situation and actors at the present time. During their first few years, and to some degree still, these Budget Committees have not been fully integrated into the fiscal process. Of this, more presently.

Certain other important factors must be included in the history of what led up to the Act of 1974, and its consequences to date.

Over a period of a number of years, the number of 'entitlements' was increased legislatively, and proposed changes in these were effectively taken out of the hands of the Appropriations Committees. The control of pensions, social security, and other funds and subsidies to persons and groups by law was automatically left to the originating legislative committees. Tactics such as these brought the present situation whereby the Appropriations Committees found their effective review jurisdiction eventually limited to as little as 25–30 per cent of the total expenditure. Contractual legislative authorizations were another way to increase the sacrosanct sector. *Fait accomplis* over spending in defense and public works were further virtual untouchables. Over-estimating of prospective revenues was a further protective device for higher spending. Also jurisdictional disputes between Appropriations and Ways and Means were unhelpful in dealing with growing deficits, and devices such as voting over-all cuts (the location of which to be determined by the President) were also tried.

Back of the difficulty lay the continued rise of special interests. Welfare claimants, grants-by-category to the states and localities (in addition to labor demands, business, agriculture, and the aged) all compounded the political problem of increasing fragmentation in Congress (see Chapter 11).

Meanwhile the two Budget Committees had entered the scene as additional 'actors'. Each was armed with an extensive and knowledgeable staff. Both were given the service of a new Congressional Budget Office, with monitoring, predictive, and 'think tank' functions. Among these functions were the provision of forecasting deficits in the annual budget, score keeping on the probable fiscal effects of new and proposed legislation, and assistance to the Budget and the other fiscal committees in the preparation of a series (a minimum of two) of joint resolutions incorporating the budget as a whole: expenditures (including tax expenditures), revenues, and the national debt. The first 'resolution', due 15 April, was assumed to be a provisional Congressional budget as of that date. A second required Congressional concurrent (both houses) budget resolution incorporating changes since the first resolution was set for 18 September. Theoretically this fixed both ceilings and floors to the budget and required specific action to break these limits. However, this reconciliation – if the subcommittees and committees on Appropriations, Ways and Means, and Finance did not, in fact, tally with the second resolution – brought negotiations among the various committees involved. These were to take place if possible by 5 September. The deadline has habitually been missed, and 'continuing resolutions' have been passed appropriating funds for the various agencies, whose subcommittees had been unable to agree with the budget resolution on their final total. They passed continued spending after 1 October, at not exceeding the rate of the previous fiscal year. This date was the beginning of the new fiscal year. The majority of the separate subcommittees' bills had not been so passed even by the *end* of 1982, and remained for either another 'continuing resolution' or action by the new Congress. The situation is not merely difficult; it is ridiculous as of this writing. It is especially difficult for those agencies that have no firm appropriations.

It should be borne in mind that Congress this past year had even given its Budget Committees a mandate to consider their *first* resolution as though it were the second, as to the fiscal 1983 budget. In the end, no less than four second budget resolutions were required, and quite possibly a fifth will be added by the new Congress that has taken over in January 1983.

Part of the difficulty is procedural. The President's budget is presented in terms both of agencies and of functions. The Appropriations Committees and subcommittees retain their practice of detailed consideration, line by line, by agencies. Debate and the Budget Committees tend to center on discussions of functions – defense, welfare, etc. 'Reconciliations' therefore are a major accounting hazard. Furthermore, jurisdictional jealousies complicate what is already complicated by the introduction of the Budget Committees as powerful new factors. The Senate Finance Committee has been especially reluctant to sacrifice its old formulas and power. Almost certainly these complications in the systems will ultimately be simplified in and by Congress. How is not easy to predict. All actors may be retained, and self-discipline may eventually speed up the process, or the beginning of new fiscal years may be again delayed – from 1 October to 1 January to give more time for deliberation.

It may be said that the plans of 1981 and 1982 were enormously frustrated by continuance and stubbornness of the depression. Together with what had been hoped for from the Reagan tax cuts in the way of enlarged consumer purchases which were not forthcoming, the depression brought a lessening of revenues and an increase in unemployment benefit costs – both entitlements and supplementary relief. All these factors lessened revenues and increased expenditures more substantially than the genuine economies (introduced by Reagan and by and large supported by Congress) could reduce other expenditures, especially during 1981. The Senate Finance Committee under the chairmanship of Senator Dole put through legislation for an eventual $100 billion increase in taxes. This it did by closing some of the 'tax expenditure' loopholes and by adding to the taxes on alcohol and tobacco. These helped, but the deficit for fiscal 1983 is still estimated to rise to possibly $200 billion unless there is a substantial improvement in the economy. The other additional tax (5c a gallon on gas) is earmarked for increasingly urgent repairs to the highway system and bridges, the remaining unconstructed portions of the Federal Highway System, and an allotment to cities toward the completion of rapid transit systems. Reagan (as of January 1983) predicts a deficit for fiscal 1984 of $189 billion even with a forecast of some recovery, a decline in interest rates in general, and on the federal debt in particular. Increased expenditure on national defense (in the absence of a meaningful arms reduction agreement) will offset some proposed expenditure freezes, further transfer of functions to the states, and other economies.

Incidentally, the part of the Reagan program involving bloc grants to states and localities by major functions has already produced some economies in federal agencies charged with enforcement of the details involved in the replaced grants-by-category. The transfer of responsibilities to the states has been costly to the latter, as the bloc grants thus far have been insufficient to cover state and local costs.

There thus remain major problems in the whole cluster of finance, unemployment, international trade, arms costs, nuclear threats, deficits and their effects. As of this writing, confidence in the Reagan leadership is waning. The elections of 1982 lessened his power with Congress. By 1984, confidence will either be restored and his re-election will follow, or a new President will take over, and his leadership is likely to last at least a year! The Presidential system faces its greatest test to date in the fiscal area. Economic rather than political forces may be the more important in determining the shape of the immediate years ahead. Unemployment has probably peaked, but this is somewhat deceptive. Employment has been reasonably static in total, as the number of additional women employed has kept fair pace with the increasing unemployment in both sexes. The fall-off in the birthrate will create a few less young people in search of work. But the effect of these demographic factors may well be less than the change in the nature of employment. The 'smoke stack industries' in the United States may continue their erosion by the cheaper labor costs elsewhere, plus the growth of robotics as an alternative to cheaper American labor. This may mean a transition from reliance on such manufacturing to a service and high technology economy.

If great fiscal deficits continue, their effects will become more and more drastic. These include dangers of increase in inflation and a growing sentiment for a constitutional amendment for a balanced budget, a revision in the budgetary process, greater cooperation between Congress and the Presidency, a disciplining of special interest claimants, reform of the financing of political campaigns, perhaps even biennial budgets. All these seem like a tangled web – but the American people are in a mood to accept strong leadership, international obligations, domestic compassion.

Reagan's fiscal 1984 Budget, unveiled the closing days of January, has received a surprisingly friendly reaction – that he had acted responsibly. Predictably many of the Democrats called for a slowdown in defense expenditures balanced by an increase in the allotments for the needy. The total budgeted expenditure came to $848.5 billion. A successful compromise in Social Security changes to establish solvency has been worked out by the leaderships of both parties. This augurs reasonably well for further bipartisan agreements in both foreign and domestic policy. The difficulties inherent in the present fiscal situation are so colossal (and worldwide) that a sober mood of compromise may prevail, especially if the signs of economic recovery multiply. Major barriers to solving these economic and fiscal crises are their world-wide nature and the absence of any general agreement among authorities in macro-economics as to how to deal with them.

13
The Instruments of International Policy

Edward S. Corwin, in his study of the Presidency, makes the following statement: 'The Constitution, considered only for its affirmative grants of power which are capable of affecting the issue, is an invitation to struggle for the privilege of directing American foreign policy.'[1] The struggle is, of course, between the President and Congress, and within Congress, involving more especially the Senate.

We may divide the relevant constitutional provisions into two groups, the direct and the indirect. The direct provisions are the following. Treaties are to be concluded by the President with the advice and consent of two-thirds of the Senate. The President is commander-in-chief of the armed services. Congress, by majority vote of both houses, declares war. Foreign commerce is one of the fields in which Congress is empowered to legislate. But there are also a number of other powers indirectly related to international policy that have had a profound effect. There is, first, the ill-defined but expansive 'executive power' of the President. There is his power to enforce laws, which includes treaties and, apparently, also international law. There is the Congressional power of appropriation and Congressional authority to pass laws in numerous fields other than foreign commerce, fields that have come to have international implications. There is also the provision that appointments, unless specifically exempted, shall be made by the President, subject to confirmation by the Senate.

If we place these various powers in pairs, it will be clearer what Corwin meant. The conclusion of treaties and the making of appointments require action by both President and Congress (i.e., the Senate in these instances). Executive power is balanced or checked by appropriations. The President's power as commander-in-chief is at least nominally offset by the power of Congress to declare war. Enforcing and passing laws, with the wide range of discretion that the contemporary type of law allows, may similarly be regarded as offsets of power.

Obviously, in such a situation, where many of the provisions are quite general or even vague in nature, precedents and Court decisions must be brought into the picture for any real appreciation of the complex situation. A few points were clarified almost immediately after the establishment of the nation. President Washington found formal association with the Senate during the negotiating stage of treaty-making too awkward, and the 'advice' part of the 'advice and consent' clause relating to treaty-making was quietly dropped. Yet, increasingly today, there is advance Presidential consultation with members and committees of both houses, and Senators and Representatives participate as delegates in international negotiations and conferences.

Of some importance was the precedent that the President might use special or personal emissaries in negotiations without their being subject to the Senatorial confirmation required of ambassadorial appointments. American representation at the Vatican has been of this character. Because ambassadorial status for such a representative would have roused religious controversy, and Senatorial consent perhaps would not have been forthcoming, the 'personal emissary' status offered a convenient device.

In the realm of legislation, Congress can repeal clauses of treaties or refuse to appropriate funds to carry out a treaty, and the executive can do nothing about it. However, neither of these contingencies has happened often. More frequently, the Senate may attach binding restrictions as part of the ratification process.

Soon after the establishment of the government, there set in a series of events or precedents that marked a long continued period of Presidential ascendancy in foreign affairs. After certain early instances to the contrary, it fairly soon became established that the President, and not Congress, was to be the vehicle of communication with foreign governments. This power was freely used for many decades as an instrument in our Latin American policy, and now figures in the struggle with world Communism.

During the American Civil War, President Lincoln stretched the executive power in a fashion that, under later Presidents, was to figure largely in international relations as well. He united the powers of commander-in-chief and enforcer of laws in his acts – blockading ports, imposing martial law and creating and punishing new offenses thereunder, excluding papers from the mails, and freeing the slaves, all without prior Congressional action.

President Wilson carried these powers further. Even though the Senate refused authorization, he armed American merchant vessels. By frequent use of troops abroad, he confirmed the distinction between acts of war and police action in defense of international law – thus unmistakeably bracketing the enforcement of international law as one of the prerogatives of his office.

President Franklin Roosevelt, bypassing the alternative use of the treaty-making procedure, traded destroyers for naval bases, occupied Greenland, concluded the Atlantic Charter, and agreed to Soviet resumption of power in Manchuria, all by executive agreement. As commander-in-chief of the armed services, he or President Truman ordered the sinking of submarines on sight, made military decisions that time has indicated in effect left large sections of Europe in the hands of the Soviets, stationed troops in Europe semipermanently, and ordered American armed forces to support the South Koreans in their resistance to North Korean aggression (subsequently converted into a United Nations police action). Under the same constitutional power, President Kennedy and President Johnson made fateful decisions concerning Laos and South Viet Nam. President Nixon, with the tacit consent of its government, bombed and fought the Communist troops in their Cambodia sanctuaries. In the enforcement – or speed-up – of the understandings presumed from the Kissinger–Le Doc Tho negotiations, he blockaded Haiphong and bombed Hanoi.

It seems clear that these powers of the President – over foreign relations, over the armed services, and his residual executive power – have in fact gravely impaired, if not invalidated altogether, the presumably exclusive power of Congress to declare war. In an affirmative sense, the power still exists, because Congress can, if it wishes, force a war on the President. In its exclusive sense, the constitutional clause is a dead letter, for Presidents can usually control events leading to the actual outbreak of hostilities, and so confront Congress with *faits accomplis.* Five out of the seven major wars in American history were associated with Presidential policies. This does not mean that Congress was reluctant when the time came or that Congress differed with the preliminary decisions – usually quite the contrary – but rather that the really critical decisions in many instances were made by the President alone.

In an endeavor to redress the balance and in reaction against the series of events leading to our Viet Nam involvement, Congress in 1974 passed the War Powers Act. Under the provisions of this Act, the President must report all uses of American troops abroad within 48 hours, together with reasons for sending them. If within 60 days Congress does not approve, the President has another 30 days to withdraw them.

Apart from use of the armed services, American foreign policy is conducted largely through several formal instruments. The four principal ones are the treaty, the executive agreement, United Nations action, and an act of Congress. Resolutions of Congress may be regarded as a special type of the last named.

The treaty, the agreement, the act are quite confused in their respective use as instruments of action, especially the first two. It seems apparent that the treaty and the executive agreement are, in point of fact, interchangeable; almost any international transaction that can be performed by one can also be performed by the other. The use of the agreement has increased tremendously, both relatively and absolutely, in recent years. This is one evidence of a trend toward the decline of the peculiar influence of the Senate – a decline measured against the power of the President on the one hand and against the power of Congress as a whole on the other. The potentialities of action of the entire Congress, as opposed to the two-thirds vote of the Senate, in treaty-making was early illustrated in the case of the annexation of Texas. The Senate refused to ratify a treaty to this effect, but Congress subsequently sanctioned it by majority vote of both houses.

The tendency to rely upon executive agreements rather than treaties has been subject to severe attack, especially in the Senate. Executive agreements of very great importance can be concluded secretly, agreements such as those at Yalta granting the Soviets important concessions at the expense of China as the price of her entry into the Pacific war.

This element of secrecy is especially frowned upon for circumventing the clear intent of the framers of the Constitution that there should be no secret treaties. However, very important matters are still handled in treaty form, and the Senate's peculiar role remains a real one.

One of the most spectacular recent developments was Nixon's almost total concentration of important decisions in the White House. The procedures associated with this were fairly elaborate, but they first involved bringing in Kissinger as the President's Assistant in National Security policy. The National Security Council [2] was made into the principal deliberative and validating instrument. It was given a fairly large expert staff under Kissinger. Memos on options in various aspects of foreign and defense goals and policy were prepared, classified as to importance and adequacy, and, if important, sent on to the President for decisions. Such decisions were then issued in the form of directives binding on all the principal actors. When Kissinger became Secretary of State, the future role of the National Security Council became uncertain. For a while, Kissinger also continued to hold the office of the President's Assistant in National Security Policy. Eventually he was replaced by General Scowcroft, but with a staff drastically curtailed in size and specialization. Ford, Carter, and Reagan continued the office, with its chief power that of immediate access to the President. The Secretary of State resumed his normal function as Cabinet chief of Foreign Policy. One anomaly remained: Reagan made Jeane Kirkpatrick, head of our United Nations delegation, a member of his Cabinet.

Thus far, the picture would appear to indicate a seemingly inexorable trend toward Presidential ascendancy or even dominance in the international field. But there are certain developments so recent and so profound that, while their long-range effects cannot yet be fully assessed, thus far they seem to have operated in the direction of a very considerable enhancement of the role of Congress as a whole, over against the role of the President or the Senate by itself. These developments are the growth of widespread popular interest in foreign affairs and the rise of the so-called total diplomacy. The two are not unrelated.

The growth of popular interest has affected Congress in obvious ways. Foreign policy is now a major issue in election campaigns; it is a frequent subject of deputations and resolutions from local organizations and of letters from constituents. Increasingly, the members of both houses are called upon to speak on the subject in their districts and states. In their day-to-day work, they themselves are increasingly aware of its enormous and often decisive importance in domestic affairs also. The schools and colleges have, for years, been emphasizing the international scene; so have the organizations for adult education and the churches. Most of all, the interest was engendered by World War II and the fact that America has been unable to extricate itself from the revolutionary consequences that have followed – a situation very different from that which prevailed after World War I. Congress, therefore, is literally compelled to take a constant and increasing interest in these affairs beyond our borders; and the powers are there under the Constitution for such interest to translate itself into effective influence.

In the second place, we are living in an era of total diplomacy. The world struggle is now no longer thought of as even primarily one ultimately to be resolved in military terms – tremendously important though these are. For the contemporary struggle is not one of nation against nation, but one in which each and every nation – those behind the Iron Curtain as well as those outside it – is internally divided, with each part having its allies and enemies in every other nation. Hence the particular group in power in a given nation more and more finds this total diplomacy necessary – to reach the peoples within and outside its own borders by economic, cultural, political, psychological, and spiritual means, as an alternative or supplement to military means. This has brought in the day of the 'program' in international affairs. As the strongest nation of the free world and hence its chief leader, America finds her policies made up largely of these programs: the Marshall Plan, technical aid, military aid, international exchange stabilization, cooperation with the World Bank, affiliates of the United Nations, and cultural exchange. These programs not only require an initial authorization by act of Congress, but even more they require Congressional action in the form of continuing appropriations.

Thus the role of Congress has again become a vital, affirmative one, not suffering too much by comparison either qualitatively or quantitatively with that of the executive. For a better understanding of this role, it is worth passing in review a number of its manifestations.

In the first place, there has come to be a definite policy of associating members of the relevant Congressional committees with many of the important negotiations leading up to the conclusion of agreements, treaties, or programs. For a considerable period before the end of World War II, the Secretary of State or his representative held more or less regular informal conferences with a number of the Senators to consult on the postwar problems and settlements. This was followed by the formal designation of ranking Senators of both parties to the London, San Francisco, and Bretton Woods conferences. Thus members of the Senate participated in the framing of the charters of the United Nations and of the International Bank of Reconstruction and Development, and Senatorial ratification was undoubtedly facilitated by this fact. Members of Congress are now frequently sent as delegates to the UN General Assembly and to other international bodies. The Conference on Peaceful Uses of Atomic Energy included several Congressmen.

In at least two important instances, Congressional support indicated in advance has given confidence to the executive, in pursuit of certain policies. These included the Fulbright and Connolly resolutions pledging support for our adherence to an international organization, and the frequent formal and informal evidences of Congressional desire to see a European federation. The measure of consolidation of opinion that followed the hearings on the dismissal of General MacArthur did something to improve the very serious lack of rapport that had previously existed between Congress and the executive regarding Far Eastern policy.

Bipartisanship has been a very striking aspect of American postwar foreign policy (to a great extent, until very recently, this has been true also of Britain), and this has been bought at a certain price. The price has been the willingness of the State Department to consult the opposition leadership in Congress – a precedent that was really established with the late Senator Vandenberg (Chairman, Senate Foreign Relations Committee, 1947–9)[3] – and to accept many of its ideas. This, too, has enhanced the role of Congress. Thus far, the bipartisan approach has largely withstood the very considerable strain to which it has been subjected – the Far and Middle East and East Asia belatedly joining Europe, Latin America, and international organizations as fields for such action. Growing differences in perception of

Viet Nam was the decisive factor in President Johnson's decision not to run for re-election. Inability of President Carter to secure the support of two-thirds of the Senate lay back of his decision not to submit the SALT II agreement for ratification. He declared it his policy to observe it as long as the Soviet Union did the same. Initially President Reagan did the same, at least until the resumption of further arms control negotiations.

Of another nature has been growth of the independent effectiveness of Congress. It had long been the usually unexpressed, but none the less deeply held, conviction of many in the State Department that inherently it possessed a virtual monopoly of wisdom and knowledge in its field – certainly more than an amateur Congress. Quite apart from the very great knowledge of foreign affairs and areas possessed by certain Congressmen, the growth of professional staffs of high competence available to the Foreign Relations, Foreign Affairs, and other committees makes this conviction no longer tenable. Congress is now in a better position to subject matters such as the SALT agreements, the international aspects of the energy crisis, or the arms and technical-assistance program to adequate independent analysis. This is certainly one way in which the growth of an independent staff has affected the balance of power between the two branches. Deeper factors than staff analyses naturally find expression in Congressional support and opposition, but these analyses focus attention on basic data in such fashion as often to prove decisive.

The acquisition of such staff aid also renders more feasible actual Congressional initiative in foreign affairs. It is always difficult to identify the crucial factors in a policy change, especially because to do so takes one into the morass of the analysis of human motives. It does seem safe to say, however, that the Congressional initiative in certain such changes preceded and probably materially influenced a subsequent shift in State Department policy. We include in this category the shift from the attempt to bring the Chinese Nationalists and Communists together toward exclusive support of Chiang Kai-shek, the shift from boycott to a measure of financial aid to Franco Spain (under some pressure from the military as well), emphasis on loans rather than grants in foreign aid, the Peace Corps, and the phasing out of our military involvement in Viet Nam. The Smith-Mundt Act of 1948, setting up an information and educational exchange program was a precursor of the subsequent restlessness in Congressional circles at the absence of a more aggressive ideological and psychological warfare. More recently there are signs of interest in the House Foreign Affairs Committee of a desire to be associated at the 'formulation of policy' stage.

Of still another character has been a certain tendency in Congress to incorporate limitations on the executive in the terms of an original act or resolution. Some of these, such as the acts authorizing the Reciprocal Trade Agreements, have consisted of time limits to prevent the use of the veto power against a repeal of the original act. In the authorization of the stationing of troops in Europe, an attempt was made to impose the obligation of consultation prior to increasing the number of troops. Some limitations find their way into the texts of appropriation bills. Congressional insistence on tying 'most favored nation' treatment for Soviet trade to a formal agreement for free emigration for Soviet Jews proved fatal to the agreement. A similar proviso cutting off military aid to Turkey unless a Cyprus agreement is reached, seemed as likely to defeat as to enhance its objective. Congress subsequently lifted the ban.

There remains also an ill-defined field of influence in which Congress – or Congressmen – can say things to other nations, in a sense irresponsibly, that the executive could not publicly say without adverse effects upon our relations. Members of Congress meeting informally at Strasbourg with unofficial representatives of European parliaments can indicate in no uncertain terms the strength of American sentiment for a federated Western Europe – without serious offense being taken, and without the overtone of undue pressure that would have attached itself to similar public statements by the President or the Secretary of State. Or, by a House amendment to an appropriation bill, Congressmen can signal their displeasure at anti-American riots or the cultivation of the opium poppy. Even the signs of random disapproval on the part of certain members of Congress have signalled to the opposition parties in the Israeli government a spreading disapproval of the slaughter of civilians in Lebanon and the bombing of West Beirut by Israeli forces. This preceded our official disapproval. By way of illustration of the diverse and broad nature of Congressional interest and influence it is illuminating to list the fields with which Congress was a factor in just one year – 1979. Those identified in the annual publication prepared by the Congressional Research Service for the Foreign Affairs Committee were the following: the SALT agreements, relations with China and Taiwan, Iran, Israel, Egypt, the Palestinians, Rhodesia, the Panama Canal, the Caribbean, Nicaragua and Cuba, Mexico, foreign trade policy, foreign aid, refugees. Many of the headings included treaties, legislation, conferences, the executive and Congress, sanctions, details of appropriations, resolutions to guide our policy, investigations, etc.[4] In other words, Congress can and does perform the role of a barometer, bringing to bear upon the policies of other nations such influence as they care to attach to American public opinion, without their seeming to have to decide under the pressure they would feel in the case of formal representations from the executive. Such influence can be in the form of a non-binding concurrent or simple resolution of Congress; it can be in floor debate. It can be upsetting or it can be constructive – but it can be ignored only at the peril of the other nations concerned.

In any general appraisal of the formulation of American foreign policy, it must be granted that the President has very great advantages. The initiative must remain primarily his. He possesses both secret and nonsecret information that flows to him with a promptness and in a quantity that Congressional staffs, however able, can never rival. As commander-in-chief, he is in a position to create situations of such compelling urgency that Congress finds a choice of alternatives denied it. He brings to this aspect of his office all the influence associated with its very great prestige. Diplomacy is his exclusive domain.

Yet Congress, the House of Representatives as well as the Senate, has comparable powers, even in the matter of initiative, and certainly in the matter of support or its refusal. Congressional intervention has been antibureaucratic in the sense that it has stressed a fresh approach to all sorts of problems. It has been an educator of the public. It has been strongly antisecret. Congressional intervention has been complicating, certainly, and, at times, irresponsibly or cavalierly exercised; but at other times, it has supported executive-sponsored programs with an enthusiasm that has lent them an authority that can only come with the knowledge of popular support. It is not without great significance that most of the major American international acts of recent years have been carried in Congress by majorities of from two to ten to one. Congress certainly delays action somewhat. Within its own membership, an inherent cleavage between the appropriations committees and the policy committees crops out from time to time. The localism of Congress shows itself in certain provisos. Yet, by and large, the past thirty-five years have witnessed a veritable revolution in American foreign policy, an assumption of responsible leadership in international affairs that few would have believed possible forty years ago, perhaps including the eventual erosion of support for Viet Nam. Relations between Congress and the executive have, on the whole, been close and cooperative in this tremendously important field. But here also the broad pattern prevails: each branch must convince the other before it can produce a major change.

A striking and courageous initiative by the President in the Middle East crisis has been his effort to establish a free Palestinian 'homeland' on the West Bank and Gaza, linked with Jordan in foreign policy and probably economics. Probably no other solution has as good a chance of eventual acceptance by all parties, especially if it is linked with an American guarantee of Israel's borders.

Then, too, there is the all-important fact that other nations are involved. Unilateral decisions on our part are no longer – if they ever were – self-executing. No analysis of the instruments of international policy is complete without some mention of the international agencies of which the United States is a member and of our allies. Days of substantially unilateral action have unfortunately not completely ended. Tremendously powerful though the American government is, it usually must pay a price to obtain its way. It is not of its nature to proceed without deference to world opinion, especially since that opinion has been organized and has found articulation in the United Nations General Assembly and Security Council. Participation in programs is increasingly channeled through international instruments, and the formulation of such programs is a cooperative process. If the United States moves less rapidly and, at times, less surely in foreign affairs than does Russia, it is not merely because its domestic government machinery must generate consensus and conviction within the nation; it is also because it is bound by agreements and by its own ethical standards to work with its associates in moving forward (or backward) in the world struggle. International (and even regional) machinery is fragile at best, but the United States is committed to using it in international policy.

14
Defense in a Nuclear Age

Until recently, the American people saw war as merely a disagreeable, albeit tragic, episode in a normally peaceful era. They were either at war or at peace. The concept that peace was nothing but war waged by nonmilitary means was completely alien to traditional American thinking. By 1960, it was clear that a profound change had come over the American national psychology. It has already been mentioned in another connection that the Americans considered themselves as being at war – in the sense that the Soviet Union willed the destruction of our institutional life by one means or another. In the preceding consideration of international policy, defense overtones were present almost throughout. Detente as of now is regarded in the United States as almost completely suspect as a viable prospect. The continuous growth in Soviet armaments, Communist policy in Afghanistan, Poland, and the Caribbean are regarded as the chief pressure points.

But its own defense is not all that matters to the United States. The United States finds itself bound by a system of military alliances to a major sector of the non-Communist world. In NATO, in particular, the fear is not so much that its allies will commit the United States as that the United States will make some move in defense or foreign policy that will commit the allies – perhaps even to their nuclear destruction. Neither the United States nor its associates can maneuver freely, which is perhaps just as well. The earlier major independent venture of the allies – the Suez attack – ended in near disaster. The immediate major points of contention involve the conflicting views and actions as to extent and nature of East-West trade, and the extent of installing the neutron bomb in Western Europe. On the other hand, mutual involvement creates tensions and frustrations of its own. There are failures to act at all through lack of unanimity. There is also the desire of allies and friends on opposite sides of what to each is a terribly important question, that the United States shall become its particular partisan – in Korea and Japan, Kashmir, Israel, Africa, Greece and Turkey over Cyprus and the Aegean, Cambodia, southern Africa, the Falklands/Malvinas, Beirut, the future of the West Bank of Jordan and Arab Jerusalem.

In the world setting, defense policy and foreign policy are obviously inseparable. Moreover, the United States is learning the hard way that far more is involved in defense than the strictly military aspects. The 'fronts' in the struggle are all-pervasive. Of the orthodox types of warfare – military, economic, political, psychological – Americans are not too badly educated as to the first two; but the second two, and especially the last, find them on the whole naive, if not illiterate. Fears and inhibitions as to possible domestic criticism render much of their psychological effort abortive. Then, too, there is an unintended defensive and international dimension to matters of domestic policy – an economic recession, racial segregation, narcotic drugs, violence, for example – that is enormously complicated. The United States is just too powerful, too universally involved, too much the object of hopes and fears throughout the world to live to itself. Millions of Americans resent this fact profoundly and look for all kinds of escapes. Millions of others see in it an opportunity and a destiny, but differ greatly as to what course of action is appropriate. The majority are probably more bewildered than indifferent, but are quick to criticize apparent failures, however much the circumstances leading to failure may have been out of the control of the nation.

The avalanche of scientific discoveries in the defense field creates a tempo in which decisions made one year are obsolete the next – but they have none the less set in motion defense activities whose momentum is arrested only with the greatest difficulty. The 'lead time' of a new defense weapon is notoriously long, but even the construction of a prototype is usually *after* a policy decision has been made. There is an analogous 'lead time' in arriving at the original decision – from the time an idea was born through the stage of analysis and clearance – and this may result in the idea itself being obsolete by the time it reaches the final board or person for decision. Then either the obsolescence is disastrously overlooked, or a whole fresh start has to be made. We shall note presently certain devices whereby attempts have been made to solve these problems. Answers are far from easy. What actually does a nation do when the capacity for mutual annihilation is already here? Or when a galaxy of alternatives for the delivery of this annihilation is on the horizon – the plane, the missile, the nuclear submarine, biological and chemical warfare, the 'suitcase' bomb with its numerous variants, the space platform, the satellite, and whatever else tomorrow and the day after may bring? The problems, for example, of civil defense, of inspection, of warning and detection, and of avoidance of accidental triggering grow in geometrical progression. The 'nuclear club' has an open-ended membership among the nations. Suppose also that a madman were to gain control of a nuclear-equipped nation. Hitler and Stalin were surely clinically mad – and they possessed virtually absolute power. Would either of them have hesitated to use nuclear weapons as the alternative to downfall, or as instruments of international blackmail? Pol Pot and Idi Amin remind us that the day of the paranoiac dictator is not yet over.

The United States has evolved a defense structure or mechanism that matches the complexity of the problem, but not its tempo. It bears witness to the need for close coordination with foreign policy; it provides mechanisms for coordination of the three great branches of the armed services; it evaluates weapons systems; it retains civilian control; it has ways whereby the right questions eventually are asked; it focuses ultimate responsibility upon the President as commander-in-chief; it provides paper plans for economic mobilization; it maintains a skeleton civil defense; it coordinates its plans with its allies – but so elaborate and inter-related are these that delays of a procedural nature constantly impair or even destroy the ultimate usefulness of the decisions, result in lost motion, create the impression of clumsiness, add to the costs, and seem at times to substitute optimistic press releases for timely achievement.

What is this structure?

Rightly and obviously, defense is centered on the President, or at least in the Presidency through his Assistant for National Security

Policy. The key role for policy planning and decision ostensibly is played by the National Security Council. The President is its chairman, and the other permanent members are the Vice-President, Secretary of State, and Secretary of Defense. Custom has also included the Director of Central Intelligence and the Chairman of the Joint Chiefs of Staff. Others may be invited when the agenda is appropriate. Deputies may, and often do, represent their principals. The Council meets often, especially in emergencies. Secrecy is naturally observed, so not too much is known as to its agenda. Generally, it appears to be concerned rather with the linkage of defense and foreign policy than with the strategy and tactics of defense itself. These latter areas are largely departmental, though often reviewed by the Council. The staff work of the Council itself is now usually performed by *ad hoc* committees set up for each major problem. If the committee is sufficiently important, it is chaired by a member of the Council; and in any event, it may call upon its own or departmental staff for research.

Responsible to the NSC is the Central Intelligence Agency, whose director normally attends the Council sessions. Digests from the CIA go daily to the principals, and special evaluations are prepared, either on the initiative of the CIA or at the request of the NSC. President Kennedy abolished the Operations Coordinating Board, which had served as the agent for seeing that the decisions of the NSC were implemented. He was known to be more than mildly skeptical of the NSC itself as an effective instrument. Initially, he appeared to be holding the Secretaries of State and Defense more or less personally responsible for coordinating with each other and with other appropriate agencies, though he himself attempted the almost impossible task of personally mastering the important issues through memoranda and *ad hoc* conferences. Following the 1962 Cuban missile crisis, however, the NSC regained much of its previous power, and President Johnson, initially at least, accorded it primary status. We have already mentioned the role assigned to it by Nixon. President Reagan seems to be making good use of it. The resignation of the knowledgeable but abrasive Alexander Haig, and his replacement by George Shultz as Secretary of State probably presents a reassuring opportunity to replace internal personal rivalries by cooperation.

The major operating agencies in the Executive Branch in the field of national security are (first and foremost) the Department of Defense and the Department of State. Extremely important are also the Department of Energy, the Arms Control and Disarmament Agency, the Agency for International Development, and the US Information Agency. Important defense responsibilities are also located in the Central Intelligence Agency, the Treasury, the Department of Justice (especially for control of subversives), the Department of Commerce, the National Aeronautics and Space Administration, and others.

The Department of Defense dwarfs all federal departments, save only the Health and Human Services. It has gone through a number of reorganizations and has now achieved stability. Perhaps its organizational problems and principles are best understood as those of the traditional services in the throes of a new strategy. It is not only that an attack (or defense) requires coordination of land, sea, and air forces. This held true during World War II. But it is also true that modern weapons systems themselves blur the old distinctions. Strategic bombing can be done by either naval or air force. Guided missiles – to which branch do they belong? The concept of gigantic, coordinated task forces or of missiles under unified command and with fused weapons is rapidly superseding the classic trio as the realistic way in which the armed services must function – and be organized as well. Subsidiary to this, but still of very great importance in terms of organization, is the question of relating civilian and military, with the ultimate control presumably lodged in the former. The reader should bear in mind that civilian control means many things, and one of its least fortunate aspects is the fact that the average tenure of an Assistant Secretary of Defense is only slightly over one year. This introduces delays without compensatory advantages. How to structure criticism and 'frontier' thinking and how to organize planning and decision-making so as to reduce the time element are other problems far from solved.

Whatever the eventual form of organization, it must in some fashion provide for all these elements. The Army, Navy, Air Force, and Marine Corps still remain as constituent units. Inter-service planning has been given more or less appropriate vehicles, headed by the Joint Chiefs of Staff. The Joint Chiefs (with or without enhanced power for their chairman) will certainly also coordinate strategy in the event of actual war. The chairman attends the meetings of the National Security Council. Centralized groups directly responsible to the Secretary of Defense have assumed functions dealing with strategic planning, foreign military assistance, research and development, manpower, logistics, international security, civil defense, military operations in outer space, weapons evaluation, health and environment, intelligence, telecommunications, joint service schools, communications, contract audit, mapping, Congressional and public relations, and nuclear matters.

The Department of Energy and the National Aeronautics and Space Administration have a dual responsibility, civil as well as defense, but much of their basic research and current procedure has strong military overtones.

Cutting across both civilian and military objectives is the International Development Cooperation Agency (of which the Agency for International Development is the core). It is closely related to the State Department. Much of its activity has been in 'defense support', comprising substantial aid to the economies and military strength of various nations so as to enable them better to carry their defense establishments.

For a while, the American effort to reduce armaments was accorded virtual Cabinet status. President Eisenhower's Special Assistant for Disarmament, Harold Stassen, met continually with the Cabinet and the National Security Council, and reported directly to the President. After Stassen's resignation, the office was downgraded, operating under the Secretary of State. The Arms Control and Disarmament Agency now technically has independent status, but is housed in the State Department building. It brought forth the first SALT agreement. The second SALT agreement has not yet been ratified by the Senate, but both nations claim to be observing it. Meanwhile, other negotiations are proceeding or scheduled. These are likely to supersede SALT II.

The Department of State and the United States Information Agency extend the scope of their efforts far beyond their undoubted defense dimension. The unending search for peace and international understanding is perhaps their principal reason for existence. Most of their overt defense moves have been by way of reaction against propaganda attacks by the other side, rather than demonstrations of initiative.

The role and methods of the Central Intelligence Agency are the subject of the most intense controversy, especially the monitoring of its covert 'black' activities or even their continuance. Committees in both houses of Congress are studying this most difficult field. The Agency itself claims to have responded to Congressional demands by acquainting these Committees – confident of their pledges of secrecy – with their various clandestine activities. Its function in preparing estimates is not in question.

To the lay public, it may seem a bit unusual to include Congress in a discussion of the organization of defense. True. Congress must appropriate. The Constitution also gives it the power 'to make rules for the government and regulation of the land and naval forces' – not by any means a self-defining provision. It gives effect to this from time to time by passing laws – usually incubated in its Armed Services Committees. It conducts a 'post audit' of failures, using its investigatory powers. Committees other than Appropriations and Armed Services assume legislative responsibility in their respective fields. Of these, the orbits of the Foreign Relations, Foreign Affairs; Energy and Natural Resources, Energy and Commerce; Commerce, Science, and Transportation; Science and Technology – the last four largely through subcommittees – all deal with subject matter vital to defense.

However, jurisdiction is of less importance than function. Congress is not too well suited to make strategic policy; it is admirably suited to evaluate such policy. In this regard, it performs something of the role of Her Majesty's Loyal Opposition in the British Government. It can and does ask the right questions; it can and does force answers. It can point out incongruities; it can spur decisions. It can do all of this by virtue of the overriding assumption that it seeks first and foremost our national strength.

So much that is vital to an understanding of the process of decision-making is classified information that one hesitates to attribute even an energizing factor to Congress in any particular instance. However, there is an impressive list of recent defense decisions and discussions which were at least preceded by strong Congressional activity in their direction. At the obvious risk of error in particulars, we might list the following as examples: possible obsolescence of bombers, a national reserves policy, the nuclear-powered submarine, the H-bomb, tactical atomic weapons, service unification, continued cost overruns, and the organization and function of the National Security Council. At present, elements in Congress are joining the President and much of the public in pressing for more serious attention to armaments reduction, for expediting the missile and outer-space programs, for stronger psychological warfare, and for nuclear-powered aircraft carriers. In America, and especially in Europe, demands for avoidance of nuclear war and reduction or abolition of nuclear weapons have reached the stage of mass demonstrations, as the consequence of a nuclear holocaust becomes obvious. The need for parallel action on the part of both superpowers gives an imperative dimension to arms reduction talks. Eventually it will become apparent that adequate mutual inspection of such agreements as may emerge is a 'must'. On the other hand, the 'state of the art' of distant detection from satellites may already be adequate.

It is relatively simple for Congress to act or to press for action in rapid fashion – as rapid as the growth of an idea in the mind of a single Senator, or the marshaling of evidence in a committee hearing, or the preparation of a staff report. No other agencies or persons need be 'consulted'; no clearances need be obtained; no inhibitions need restrain. In these regards – given its function as critic – Congress is better suited to move quickly than is the cumbersome inter-departmental organization of the Executive. Budgetary restraints are also growing.

Nor is this the only role of Congress. Until recently, by the time an important decision reached the President, more likely than not the 'considerations adverse' and the alternatives had been filtered out somewhere along the line. The 'position paper', or brief, was reduced to a marshaling of evidence in such a fashion as to support the action proposed. Eisenhower, when Chairman of the Joint Chiefs of Staff, used structured units to criticize ideas and to assess their probable effects on strategy after a given number of years in the future. However, since the beginning of the Kennedy Administration, dissenting as well as supporting data have often been put before the President. Nixon insisted upon options. Yet, conventions of secrecy muzzle public expression of differences of opinion, and, at least nominally, the executive must give the impression of being monolithic on the matter. It is at this point that Congress claims the role or even the duty of laying bare the *total* picture. From tips on the part of those who were overruled in process, from military critics in private life, from its own knowledge or its own staff and support agencies come the incentives to probe and probe deeply. Many of the original decisions had been and still were correct. Others were correct at the time, but had become obsolete while the interests vested in their retention were as yet too strong to allow a reconsideration within the defense organization itself. Still others were wrong from the beginning. In any event, a lively and up-to-date audit can be generally salutary, however much it may be resented by those affected. Recent history records Congressional investigations fully as often vindicating major executive decisions in the defense field as suggesting their alteration – but alteration can be particularly important in this day and age when meteoric changes in one sector send their reverberating waves of change through all the other sectors, with a cavalier disregard of vested interests on the way.

Two other vital elements in the defense structure must be noted to complete the picture. Enormously strong though the United States is, it has chosen and chosen rightly to make common cause with others in the free world. Its important defense and foreign-policy decisions must be made in conjunction with at least its stronger allies in NATO and Japan, and a number of regional decisions must be worked out with its Latin American, ASEAN, and ANZUS associates. But so must the allies reciprocate with the Americans. All this is complicating, and certainly accounts for much apparent delay and indecision. Then, too, the United States is a member of the United Nations and is pledged to take it into account in defense as well as in its other policies. The United States has renounced all except peaceful means in pursuit of national policies – save only in response to an overt attack upon itself or upon one of those with whom it has made common cause. Whatever else this means, it at least means that the enemy is granted the advantage of surprise initial attack, and defensive plans must be made accordingly.

Such are the principal agencies concerned with national defense. How, then, does policy actually emerge? It would be giving a totally false impression if one were to attempt to enunciate a single formula. Rather, it is more enlightening to point to certain prevailing characteristics.

In the first place, most important policies in the past were, in fact, interagency in their evolution. The original idea may have emerged from a single agency, but an unbelievably complex network of clearances and committees bears witness to the multitudinous aspects of even a single decision. This rather than bureaucratic timidity, probably contains the principal explanation for what appears at times to Americans, as well as to other peoples, as an endemic indecision. It may well be this type of situation that gives American foreign and military policies the appearance of agitated reactions to crises, rather than affirmative and constructive moves. In military aid, as in foreign aid generally, the planning phase frequently takes longer than the actual execution, which may be obsolete politically or militarily before the event.

The Reagan leadership has introduced new factors. His proposed increase in military spending has thus far met with an adequate degree of bipartisan Congressional support. At the same time, through persuasion and economic sanctions, he is entering vigorously into arms reduction talks, starting from the 'zero option' in intermediate range nuclear weapons fixed upon Western Europe or stationed there as well as upon intercontinental missiles. Simultaneously, he is supportive of the proposed Constitutional amendment requiring a balanced budget; subject only to its breaking by a 3/5 recorded vote in both houses of Congress in case of a national emergency.

Within the capital city of each nation, the entire American 'team' of representatives – economic, diplomatic, cultural, and military (where we have a military mission) – is under the direction of the ambassador as 'head of the mission'. Where this coordination is firm and imaginative, the impact is excellent. But the 'home base' in Washington may or may not move with similar rapidity and effectiveness. The interagency deliberation overseas may or may not be matched by effective coordinating instruments at home – or vice versa.

How far the temporary conjunction of Kissinger and Nixon may have permanently affected this earlier pattern is too early to predict. The Office of National Security Advisor in the White House seems to be a fixture.

Another characteristic of the defense organization is the presence of planning based upon military intelligence and research. In the military structure, a conscious effort is made to release certain personnel from the normal line of command to do such planning. Contrary to the popular view, there is a great deal of built-in criticism in defense organization. Some is within the Department itself. Some is by contract with outside research and planning organizations, to whom questions and problems are posed. In an atmosphere fully free from any interest vested in the past, they evaluate existing strategy and explore new frontiers.

Less reassuring is the previously mentioned tendency to 'screen out' dissent in the course of policy formulation. This is seen in its most acute and serious form by the time a policy recommendation reaches the top echelon, especially the President himself. Thus, to an almost inevitable degree of obsolescence in the factors considered in the early stages, is added an oversimplification in the final stage that can be serious, if not disastrous. It is this fact that adds importance to the role of Congress as critic. To Congress go the disgruntled and the skeptics from within and outside the government. They carry ideas running the gamut from the pathological to the devastatingly acute. Each has its 'day in court', and in the pitiless light of a Congressional investigation, the total picture eventually emerges in some fashion or other. A skilled Congressional staff accelerates the process. The ultimate defense policy adopted in the executive branch in a particular situation may or may not be changed thereby, but not infrequently it is so changed. The selfsame ideas that are aired in Congress have probably been voiced at some stage in the executive policy-planning sessions, but many of them have long since filtered out by the time of final decision. Thus does the Constitution provide a corrective for still another of the faults inherent in large-scale bureaucracy.

Public opinion naturally plays a role, but of late there has been such coincidence between the official and the popular views of our national objectives, and such general bewilderment on the part of the public at large as to the tactical and strategic ways and means of attaining them, that strictly military aspects have been rather generally left for the executive and Congress to determine. The events of recent decades have muted most criticism of military expenditures except for gross cost overruns of original estimates. Actually, criticism of inadequacy rather than of expense has been the prevailing post-Sputnik note. Such influence as public opinion has exerted has been concerned with this factor and with the pros and cons of the defense aspects of foreign aid. Here, xenophobia and a world orientation have battled it out and affected programs and expenditures. Of late, the catastrophic implications of nuclear warfare have also entered the sphere of public discussion.

So, in broad outline, the defense policies, strategy, and tactics of the United States are determined. Britain can afford to confine herself to a nuclear deterrent because American strength can play for her a role akin to that which the British Navy played for America's Monroe Doctrine in a simpler age. There is no American dictator to determine a change of policy overnight, though an American President can decide in a matter of hours, if need be, to send troops to the rescue of a South Korea or a South Viet Nam, or to block a Communist takeover in, say, the Dominican Republic. We can respond quickly to a crisis; our system is less happy in its adaptability to continuous and accelerating change.

15
Political Parties

Among the several aspects of American government perplexing to British observers, none is more perplexing than the American party system. The British, with their long tradition of two major parties, find nothing incongruous in a fairly wide span of opinion within a party, but they expect a clear division of views between the parties. Even more to the point, they expect party loyalty in Parliament to assure support for measures decided upon by the party leadership, for the heart of parliamentary government has come to be party responsibility – and the penalty for marked deviation is apt to be political suicide or, at least, ostracism. Recent voting statistics would indicate relatively little fluidity among the voters supporting the Labour and Conservative candidates, although some from both parties have shifted to the as yet untried Social Democrat-Liberal coalition. Displeasure is as likely to be registered by not voting at all as it is by change of party.

Yet since about 1879 some subtle and not so subtle changes have appeared in the hitherto conventional party behavior in Parliament. Some of it has been associated with the extreme wings of the major parties – right, with the Conservatives, left with Labour. As of 1983 the latter seems to have so threatened to become the controlling element, as to lead to a substantial defection to form a new party, the Social Democrats. A substantial group of voters (hitherto Conservative) have also defected in the same direction, though defection among Conservative Members of Parliament has thus far been minimal. A Social Democrat-Liberal understanding is emerging, though not yet formalized. These developments were preceded by increasing tolerance of single issue defections or abstentions on the part of individual MPs of both major parties on emotionally charged issues, such as immigration, acceleration of socialism (the Tribune group of Labour), devolution (e.g., for Scotland or Wales). Until the advent of Social Democrats, such deviations (even though in earlier days they might have produced the resignation of the 'government' or the call for a new election) were more likely in recent years to involve a vote of 'no confidence', with the 'errant' members of both parties joining ranks with their party, and the 'government' continuing.

The supreme example – which endangered a fatal split, in both major parties, was the question of joining the European Common Market. This was settled by a popular referendum. Both parties then resumed their customary solidarity.

The author wonders if what is happening may be the search for a way in which parties may hold their ranks in government and opposition but allow an increasing amount of individual freedom when the number of major issues has so multiplied that there is no 'common denominator' either for or against many of these issues, so that parties can no longer present a 'common front'. In the United States the right of an individual in a multi-issue political spectrum (under separation of powers) has been able to allow individuals to vote their intelligence and/or conscience without sacrificing party membership. The reverse side of the coin is obviously a decline in party responsibility.

In America it seems that almost one-third of the voters classify themselves as 'independents',[1] and a large number of others do not hesitate to cross party lines to vote for candidates of the other party. The essentially nonpartisan character of much of the Congressional voting has already been noted. Even Congressional support of the President is not infrequently found from among those of the opposite party. In part, this reflects the basic 'mainstream' of American thought, which is found in both parties.[2]

In both nations, a certain inexorable trend seems to cause public support in each to gravitate normally toward two major parties. There have been and are other parties, but once it is clear to the voters which of three rival parties are the two strongest, there has been a fairly rapid disintegration of sizable support for the remaining one. It is usual to ascribe this phenomenon primarily to the single-member constituency and to simple majority elections – an indication that individuals hate to waste their votes on hopeless chances. The British system in which a Parliamentary candidate must poll a certain percentage of the votes or forfeit a deposit is not practiced in America, but the results of elections are not dissimilar. The machinery whereby the President is elected undoubtedly tends to the same end.

It is a temptation in the United States to say that there is no real difference between the Democrats and the Republicans. The element of truth in this lies in the fact that exponents of almost any 'respectable' point of view on any issue can in fact be found within the ranks of both parties. We have already seen the effect of this in Congress, where until recently partisanship has played a relatively minor role on the majority of issues and where, almost without exception, a substantial percentage of each party is found on each side of controversial issues.

There have been times when party was much more significant than at present. From the earliest years, the centralizing, aristocratic approach of Alexander Hamilton and the decentralizing popular approach of Thomas Jefferson have divided men, and the Federalist-Democratic (first called Republican) cleavage had at least occasional similarity to the cleavage between what were subsequently the two major parties. Yet a strong conservative element from the South established itself within the Democratic Party, and the Whig and later the Republican parties usually sought wide and popular roots as part of their basis for support. Under Abraham Lincoln and Theodore Roosevelt, the Republican Party found its White House standard-bearer carrying the torch of liberalism, while the conservative leaders were among the Democrats. The Democratic Party is the party of longest continuity. Its great Presidents – Jefferson, Jackson, Cleveland, Wilson, Franklin Roosevelt, Truman – have all been men who placed an accent on the progress of the common man, often against the opposition of many in Congress of their own party. Kennedy and Johnson have followed this tradition. If, since the Civil War, one Democratic base has historically been in the conservative South, the other has been among the masses and foreign-born of the great cities. In recent years, when leadership has arisen that joined these two bases of support with the radicalism of the frontier and the rise of the West, it has been able to gain power.

Yet the Republican Party, in its origin, owed much to the free air and thought of the West, and it has never quite lost this strand in its history, even when the business interests of the East joined with the conservative rural areas of the East and Middle West to gain control of the Presidency and the Congress during most of the last thirty years of the nineteenth century. When business groups lost control under Theodore Roosevelt, it was from within the party, not outside, that their privileged position was successfully attacked. Until 1930, Republican administrations had succeeded in attaching to themselves a large measure of the credit for national prosperity, and this factor, among others, gave them a considerable following among labor.

Since 1932, new factors have appeared to be operating. Two liberal and strong-minded Democratic Presidents, Roosevelt and Truman, set the pace in government intervention in economic affairs on behalf of agriculture and labor. This pace, particularly in the area of social progress, has been so rapid that a considerable measure of support within the South has been alienated – though the South's recent desertion to Eisenhower, Nixon, and Goldwater does not yet necessarily indicate that it has found its way into the Republican Party, especially as regards Congress. Conversely, the mere fact that the party out of power regards criticism as a major function has in itself resulted in associating conservatism more and more with Republicanism. Whatever the reasons, the Republican Party has steadily lost ground in terms of numbers of voters indicating a preference for it. Although it was once normally the majority party, it now has a very decided minority status. Public-opinion polls indicate that the great majority of the independent voters are moderate and liberal in their orientation. Because of this, the Republican Party, while predominantly conservative in Congress, especially in the House of Representatives, has tended to name as its Presidential candidates men from its more liberal wing, or even from outside party politics altogether (such as Willkie and Eisenhower). In this way, it hoped to tempt the independent voter and recover some of its lost strength. Only the absence of a really strong alternative contender, in a sense, gave the nomination to Goldwater in 1964.

The 1974 congressional elections brought very considerable further losses to the Republicans. The misdeeds of the Nixon administration and the stagflation in the nation as a whole undoubtedly were the major contributing factors. Yet of the thirty House Republicans who were defeated for re-election, twenty-nine were from the conservative wing.

Are there then any nationwide issues that today really divide the two parties along party lines? For years, a protective tariff filled this role, but there are now strong protectionist elements among the Democrats, and the Republicans have attracted a strong following along the Eastern seaboard whose prosperity is associated with an expanding foreign trade. Agriculture knows no party line; neither does international cooperation; nor public power; nor antimonopoly; nor even organized labor; nor universal military training; nor social security; nor public housing. These are controversial issues, and the majority sentiment of the two parties may frequently be found on opposite sides – but always there is a substantial minority of each party opposing not so much the other party as its own leadership on the particular issue.

Why is this so? We have already suggested that the two principal factors are the multiplicity of issues without a common denominator and the fact that party organization is predominantly *local*. The national stage is set by the fact that the independent executive elected for a fixed term allows party independence in Congress without the government falling, as it would in the House of Commons.

As to the multiplicity of issues, we have already spoken of this at some length. The same absence of a logical common party denominator that we have noted in Congress has its counterpart in an electorate increasingly independent and disposed to place its confidence in a *man*, rather than in a *party*. With so many issues and with the virtual impossibility of finding a party whose position (if it has taken a position, which is doubtful) on all these issues coincides with his own, the voter has partly subconsciously and partly consciously grasped the fact that perhaps he is better off if he elects the man of greater integrity and ability, for such a man will then use his judgment and do what he thinks is right. This must not be pressed too far, for even this man must not do too great violence to what is *locally* important, nor can he be too far 'out of line' with middle-of-the-road opinion on whatever are the really outstanding national issues that hold the center of attention at a given moment.

For many decades a fair number of professional political scientists have joined a fraction of party leaders in asserting that there is or should be a difference between the two parties that extends across the nation and at all levels of government. Usually, this group attempts to force the Republicans into the equivalent of 'conservatives' and the Democrats of 'liberals'. Most big city Republicans and Southern Democrats have generally refused to accept this. I knew intimately a Republican Congressman who in alternate elections classified himself as a 'liberal conservative' and 'conservative liberal'; Eisenhower spoke of himself as 'conservative in fiscal matters', a 'liberal as regards people's welfare' – incidentally not a bad formula for most candidates! More usually in both parties are those in closely contested states and districts who covet the characterizations of 'mainstream', 'moderate', 'pragmatic'.

Has the election of Reagan made a difference? There are some signs of this, but defections to the other party of the more liberal members among the Republicans and the more conservative among the Democrats have been relatively few. Direct primary balloting this year in states such as New Jersey, Texas, Vermont, South Carolina, Oregon, and even California and Florida indicate this. The landslide victory of Reagan indicated widespread shifts toward a more responsible fiscal policy, rather than inhumanity toward the masses and minorities. The Democrats, with much budgetary evidence on their side, are trying to pin the label of the 'party of the rich' on the Republicans and to claim for themselves a monopoly of 'concern for the minorities and the poor'. The weakness on both sides is the inability to come up with a sustainable fiscal policy or working and politically acceptable remedies for the existing depression, high interest rates, unemployment, the fiscal 'burdens' of the 'entitlement programs', the fiscal dilemmas of most of the state and local governments.

The localism of party organization deserves close attention. It will be remembered that, by and large, the Constitution left election laws to the states. When parties were organized, they eventually came into the orbit not of national but of state regulation. For the most part, this has meant, because of either party by-laws or state laws, that parties have been built from the local unit up through the state to the nation, rather than in the reverse order. Local units differ from state to state, but the city and county party organizations have tended, fairly generally, to be the ones with the greatest vitality. State organizations have been made up mostly of delegates from these local units, and the national committees are made up of state delegates.

There was a time when the city and county organizations almost universally were interested chiefly in 'spoils'. These consisted of jobs, immunities, favors in contracts or tax assessments, either for members of the organization or for others prepared to pay the organization for them. This is still to some extent true in many of the cities and counties. For example, many local police forces and most county sheriffs' offices are still run in part as adjuncts to a local party organization. It has been and still is an uphill fight to emancipate these local communities from even the more sinister aspects of the party machine. Hence the association, in the minds of so many Americans, of reform and nonpartisanship, and the ugly color attached historically to the term 'politician'. The much higher tone of British party organization makes its American counterpart difficult to understand. The undoubted gains in the tone of public opinion in America have in part been in the increase of independence and in part within the party organizations themselves. When evil situations become known and dramatized, the initial public response is almost always that of shock and clamor for reform – though at least partial retrogression subsequently is disturbingly frequent. Gains in the science of public administration and the professionalization of a high percentage of municipal employees have added their very great share to the improvement of government, usually a more permanent achievement than 'shock and reform'.

In any event, where party lines remain in local government and in state government (where they are almost universal), party organizations normally work and work hard for the election of their candidates. Thus a network of *local* issues, largely without national counterparts, presents itself to the electorate – still further to complicate and weaken the pattern of national party loyalty. An independent or liberal can defeat nominees of both major parties for Mayor of New York City. Until recently, California could even nominate the same man for governor on both tickets.[3] States may vote one way for state and local candidates and the other for President. In the South, until recently, factions – either personal or of differing orientation – within the

Democratic Party took the place of the two parties elsewhere. However, outside the deep South and the new state of Hawaii, there are no more than three or four states that have not elected governors from both parties in the past twenty-five years; moreover, elections in the larger municipalities are apt to be quite closely contested.

The concern of these state and local party organizations is still predominantly in the success of the candidates for state and local offices, but there are also national candidates to be nominated and elected. The interest of the local party organization in the election of these Representatives and Senators, and even of the President, is usually distinctly subsidiary to its interest in state and local successes. Nevertheless, for voters in general, the nomination by a party of strong and acceptable men for these national offices strengthens the probability of additional votes for the local candidates of the party – and vice versa. Hence there develops an inherent unwillingness to nominate or to see nominated for these national offices men whose points of view on *locally* important issues go too strongly counter to local sentiment. In the South in 1948, this went so far as to cause a rebellion within the Democratic Party that took four states away from Truman and gave them to a Southern Dixiecrat candidate.[4] As regards Representatives and Senators, the problem is distinctly easier. It is resolved by the nomination of *locally* acceptable men, largely without reference to what might be regarded as the dominant viewpoint of the party nationally. Few are the sanctions that the relatively weak national organization could bring to bear on a local party organization, even if it wished to do so – and it seldom does. It could only, under normal circumstances, assure the election of a member of the opposite party, if it did in some fashion succeed in securing the nomination of a nationally acceptable candidate who was out of line with local sentiment. With Congress organized on party lines – though not voting on them – this might bring the further penalty of loss of a majority.

Moreover, in the majority of the states, the nominating process is itself largely in the hands of the voters in what is known as the 'direct primary'. In these states and local units where the latter are partisan, by petition of a certain number of voters, any eligible person may be entered as a candidate for a party nomination for an office. On primary day – which is really a preliminary election to determine who is to be nominated – the voters of each party choose their candidates. Under these circumstances, even if the local party organization were disposed (and it usually is not) to nominate candidates for Congress who deviated sharply from the local point of view, in the interest of national party solidarity, the voters themselves would most probably defeat the attempt and nominate a man more nearly to their liking. Under these circumstances, there is no way a national party organization can be sure of defeating local 'insurgency'.

Hence the system of state and local party control, together with the direct primary, weights the scales in Congress heavily in the direction of a sprinkling of *both* parties on the side of any point of view on an issue strongly felt by a *particular region*. Public power and irrigation are widely and strongly supported in the West. The St Lawrence Seaway was supported in the states bordering the Great Lakes, while it was opposed in New England and the Lower Mississippi Valley because of fear that commerce would be deflected. Silver subsidy attracts the Rocky Mountain states, and parity of price for farm products unites agriculture in the Middle West. Strong support for collective bargaining and organized labor characterizes both parties in most industrial areas. The Eastern seaboard states favor foreign trade. The West Coast is concerned that our policy in the Far East be strong. Agrarian radicalism is strong in North Dakota and Minnesota. The South opposes social equality for the Negro. These are the *local* roots of similarities between representatives of both parties from the same region; they account for intraparty deviations nationally. Platforms are couched in terms to offend no one, except that the record of the party in power is sharply criticized by the opposition. Their convenient vagueness maintains the uneasy coalitions of state and local organizations sufficiently to conduct a Presidential campaign once every four years. Between these campaigns, the national party organizations usually sink into obscurity, and the center of the stage is assumed by the partisans in the executive branch and in Congress.

The roots of the parties and the rivalries between them are thus much more organizational than ideological. True there is much bargaining on a national scale with the great groups of labor, agriculture, and industry – and this has some ideological overtones. Yet the roots remain local. Each city precinct, each small rural area usually has its party delegate or committeeman – and often a committee as well. The municipal and county units have their party committees and their central core of leadership – one man or a few. So the organization builds up to the state and eventually to the national levels.

It is this solid core of organization that largely explains the abortive nature of the attempts of third parties to gain any solid footing. In 1912, the Progressives, under Theodore Roosevelt, polled more votes nationally than the Republicans, but within two years they were a spent force because of lack of basic local organization. For a while, the American Labor Party maintained a somewhat effective organization in New York City, but there its influence ended, and it has now all but vanished. There are a half-dozen small parties claiming national support, but it is unusual for any of them to poll even 1 per cent of the vote. If any one of them shows signs of substantial growth, one or both of the other major parties make a bid for the support of those attracted to it by espousing or seeming to espouse the issue that constituted the attraction. Historically, this has been the role of the third party – to force the adoption of an issue by one of the two major parties.

Some comment is in order as to the extent of nonvoting. After this phenomenon is fully discounted in terms of unavoidable absenteeism or lack of residential or other voter qualifications, it still remains deeply disturbing.

The one-sidedness in certain areas is a factor from time to time in nonvoting. Closely contested elections almost always bring out a larger vote. In the years before national legislation opened voting in the South to the blacks, the real contests in that region were in the Democratic primaries where the whites concentrated. It was exceptional for the Republicans to compete successfully. Now that the reason for racial party concentration is no longer much of a factor, the two-party system has made notable gains.

The absence of identifiable differences in points of view of candidates is doubtless a further factor in nonvoting. Perhaps one element of nonvoting is the discovery by the electorate that much of the really effective political action lies outside the realm of voting and expresses itself in joining in organized pressure on the officeholder once he is elected. Decline in party loyalty and growth in voter independence may make for a smaller percentage of voters, but also for greater exercise of intelligence. Some of the earlier, larger voting figures were certainly 'padded' by election frauds of one type or another. The author knows of some earlier instances of 110 per cent of those eligible voting. Studies of nonvoting have been made; and in the end, they all add up chiefly to a picture of civic indifference on the part of 10 to 50 per cent of the electorate. Single issue Political Action Committees (PACs) are normally bipartisan in their gifts to the campaign funds of the committee or subcommittee members most important to their issue.

What, on balance, may be said of the American party system? Obviously, its apparent failure to crystallize nationally on clear-cut issues or orientation has been subject to very considerable criticism. Allegations of party irresponsibility have been leveled at Congress in particular in this regard. In many quarters, the British system is held up as a shining example of what party government ought to be. Yet there is a case on the other side. Because of the very lack of clear-cut divisions, American Presidential candidates normally address their appeals to all groups, and such a campaign is nationally unifying, rather than divisive. The nomination of Goldwater from the right and McGovern from the left were disasters for their respective parties. Even the British system divides the electorate largely along class lines, and the Continental parties are much worse in this respect. Within the electorate and within Congress, the lack of party discipline makes much more feasible the exercise of individual integrity and intelligence than does a system in which rigid party loyalty on issues is the price paid for success – and the issues are really too many for this to be without its penalty in the individual's conscience. Finally, the system is locally adaptable to the continuation of the two-party system, with its advantage of constant presentation of alternative candidates. Where this is no longer so, the two party system has largely been replaced either with genuine contests in the primaries or with growth of complete nonpartisanship in local government (especially in the West).

The Americans in general feel the present system is serving them increasingly well, and they are not likely to change it fundamentally.

16
The Judiciary

True to the political theory of its age, the Constitution took cognizance of the judicial power as the third member of the governmental trinity and provided for a Supreme Court. Other federal courts it left for Congress to determine. Territorial and District of Columbia courts were included in the Congressional jurisdication by virtue of general Congressional power over territories and the seat of the government.

Each state also has its own system.

The unwritten power of federal Courts to declare a law unconstitutional is paralleled by a similar power – written or unwritten – in each state as regards its own constitution.

Except for Louisiana, where the Napoleonic Code is the basis of its jurisprudence, each state inherits the tradition and practice of the English Common Law. This it supplements or supersedes by its own statute law. Nowhere is there the juristic equivalent of the Continental *droit administratif* and its hierarchy of administrative tribunals. Yet the nature of modern government and the growth of regulatory commissions have made the practical differences less sharp than the juridical differences.

The British and other Europeans are always intrigued by the power of the American Supreme Court to declare a law unconstitutional, but they do not always understand how a case reaches the Court. The Court has consistently refused to issue advisory opinions. Consequently, there must be a party of interest to challenge the constitutionality of a law *in toto* or in part. This means that its enforcement must have commenced. A lower federal court, or even a state court, may pass on the constitutionality of a federal law, but appeals are usually taken and the case eventually reaches the Supreme Court. It should be noted that such disallowance was rare until after the Civil War. During the first eighty years of government under the Constitution of 1789, only in the key case of *Marbury v. Madison*[1] and in the Dred Scott decision[2] were federal laws disallowed. Since then, about one hundred acts of Congress have been invalidated in part or in their entirety. State laws have eight times as frequently been the subject of Supreme Court disallowance.

Because several of the cardinal economic measures of the New Deal were thrown out by the Supreme Court, in 1937 President Roosevelt made his proposal which came to be known as the 'court-packing bill'. Under this measure, he would have been empowered to appoint an additional judge for each sitting judge who had passed the age of seventy. The motive was so obvious and the sense of propriety of so many was so outraged that the measure never passed. However, the move seemed to have an effect, for certain judges voluntarily retired and others were apparently more receptive to the extensive economic controls subsequently instituted. In these and other economic issues, the problem facing the Court, broadly speaking, was usually the same as it had been down through the years: whether to follow precedents based on police power and allow extension of the sphere of governmental action, or to choose the line of decisions emphasizing the 'due process' clause, which led toward restraints on governmental regulation.

It is fairly generally realized that the Court is never rigidly bound by precedent. Nor is it necessarily held to the letter of the original intent of the Constitution itself or of its amendments – even assuming such an intent is clear, and it often is not. We have already called attention to the Court's view of its own function as that of giving effect to the continuing long-range trends in popular government.[3]

So it has changed in its view of racial equality. No longer may 'separate but equal' schools be regarded as conforming to the 'equal protection of the laws' clause of the Fourteenth Amendment. Segregation is itself discrimination, and the Court has prodded a reluctant sector of the nation in the direction of integrating its schools, its transportation, and its recreational facilities.[4] Resistance, even violent resistance, still exists in many quarters, including Boston and Detroit, but time and the traditional rule of law are on the Court's side, and the question is not 'Whether?' but 'When?' A vindication of the Supreme Court's judgment of the times is the fact that Congress passed the far-reaching Civil Rights Act of 1964 by a large majority; this Act included the controversial public-accommodations clause.

Racial equality is not the only controversial and emotionally charged issue on which the Court has ruled in recent years. The earlier emphasis on protection of property has, of late, given way to an implicitly greater emphasis on liberty of the person. In its provision of safeguards of the judicial process, in its curbing of what it deemed excesses in Congressional investigations, in its disallowing of laws designed (in its opinion) to carry too far the precautions against subversive activities, the Court has revealed what is essentially the same attitude toward the rights of individuals that it has demonstrated in the blows it has struck for racial equality.

The most recent decisions with far-reaching implications have been those invalidating the unequal apportionments in districting for state legislatures and for the House of Representatives. Until the Court intervened with these decisions, it appeared that the entrenched power of the rural areas would remain dominant indefinitely. Now, 'equal protection of the laws' has been redefined as essentially 'one man, one vote', or equal representation for each man.

Criticisms of these decisions – and of the broader trends and objectives of which they are evidence – have been in part substantive, in part couched in terms of legal principle. The fact of the matter is that the warp and woof of society today is incredibly complicated and interlocked. In such a milieu, principles are at hand for either side of almost any question – principles not only from the less complicated past, but also from the living, changing present. The Court has been accused of being 'sociological' rather than judicial in its emphasis on the present rather than the past, even though *stare decisis* remains a powerful factor.

A society so dynamic calls for creative jurisprudence; and the conscience of a nation must speak in context. The Court is but one organ of government and must respond to social change. Even so, it is the organ that by safeguards of tenure, fashion of appointment, and a great and prestigious history has created expectations, largely realized, of an aloofness, integrity, and wisdom over and above that of the other branches of the federal government. For this very reason, it is too simple to say that the Court follows the election returns. On the other hand, the Court does strive to reveal that combination of continuity and change which makes for stable progress in government at its best. This has been the conscious goal of those who, in a peculiar sense, are the guardians of an ever-living Constitution that is amended far more frequently by judicial process than by legislative action. The criticism of today becomes the accolade of tomorrow to the extent that the Court keeps faith with the ideals it has set for itself, and gauges direction as well as foundation. So the United States has sought, on the whole successfully, to forge a system of government that combines the representation of the immediate will of the people for action with the effective wisdom of those above the immediate battle.

Federal courts handle, in addition to questions of constitutionality, certain fairly well-defined types of cases. These include offenses against federal law or treaties and civil cases arising under federal law or treaties. They also include disputes between states and between citizens of two different states, and controversies to which the United States is a party. Cases involving admiralty and maritime jurisdiction and cases to which a foreign nation or citizen is a party are also subject to federal jurisdiction. So are ambassadors, ministers, and consuls. Under the Eleventh Amendment, the first to be adopted after the new republic had begun to function, no state may be sued by an outsider – either from another state or from abroad – without its own consent. The reader should bear in mind that the great majority of federal cases are settled in the lower courts. Only a few appeals to the Supreme Court are heard as of right. Most of the cases on appeal are heard by the Court's consent – that is, the consent of at least four out of nine members – on a writ of *certiorari*. The area of the Supreme Court's original jurisdiction is quite limited – to cases involving ambassadors, treaties, the states, and a few other instances.

The federal court system provides for two levels of courts inferior to the Supreme Court and for certain special tribunals.

Over the nation, there are at present some ninety federal district courts of original jurisdiction. The next level provides for eleven circuit courts of appeals. Of the latter, that of the District of Columbia performs an especially important function in the appeals it hears from the decisions of regulatory commissions and departmental tribunals.

Also established are a federal court of claims, to hear claims against the federal government; a court of customs; a court of customs and patent appeals; a tax court; and a civilian court of military appeals to hear appeals from military courts-martial.

A complete picture would include in the federal system the various regulatory commissions and the tribunals within the departments and agencies, which have already been noted.[5]

The growth of administrative law from them, generally speaking, parallels that of Britain. The problem of distinguishing between law and fact has proved central in both nations. In both, there has been a strong trend toward allowing the administrative decisions on questions of fact to be final. American jurisprudence has, however, seemed to be somewhat more concerned than has the British that the procedure by which these facts were ascertained was judicial in temper.

The Supreme Court also exercises supervision over the administration of the lower federal courts. It does this through an administrative officer, who with Court support (including the senior circuit judges) works continuously toward expediting the handling of cases and strives for businesslike and economical staffing of auxiliary personnel. In fact the question of the administration of justice generally is approaching something of a crisis: the Chief Justice has made this one of his chief concerns. Litigation and crime have greatly increased. Neither the number of judges, the legal procedures, nor the capacity of the prisons are adequate. Excessive plea bargaining and paroles are unsatisfactory adaptations. The end is not in sight.

All federal judges are appointed by the President with the approval of the Senate. Their appointments are for life or during good behavior, and are customarily, but not exclusively, partisan. Expansion of personnel is thus more likely when one party controls both branches. A liberal pension system has been introduced to stimulate retirement of judges before they suffer from senility or impairment of judgment.

Each state has its own separate judicial system. There is no uniformity, but there are certain generalizations that can be made. Each state has a 'supreme court', though it is not always formally designated as such. It also has inferior courts on one or more levels. At the lowest level – the city, county, or town – are the courts for the day-to-day petty offenses or cases. Many cities have established specialized courts at this level. Small claims, juvenile problems, marital relations, settlement of estates, and traffic offenses are the subjects most frequently segregated from the ordinary run of cases and given the benefit of special handling.

It is almost universal in the United States to pay judges. In a number of the minor or local courts, the load of cases is such that a part-time judge can handle them. There is no uniformity as to term or method of selection. Many states elect their judges at all levels. In others, appointment is general. Some use both methods. Fixed terms are usual, but life appointments or appointments subject to a compulsory retirement age are not unknown. The tone of the lower courts leaves much to be desired in many communities. Too often, they are adjuncts to the party machine, and justice is tempered or affected accordingly.

Apart from the Supreme Court, which with ephemeral exceptions is generally venerated, the American judicial system has been subjected to some fairly severe criticism. Federal judges are too often, in practice, political nominees of Senators or party organizations, and they may or may not be eminently qualified. The situation in the states, particularly at the lower levels, is often much worse. It seems difficult to obtain a conviction of a politically powerful member of the underworld or of the political bosses' henchmen. The police and prosecuting attorneys must share the blame for this.

Procedure is criticized as costly, slow, complicated, and often defeating the ends of justice. Waves of indignation, especially in response to increases in serious crime, attract attention. This at times takes the form of greater emphasis on a speedy trial, coupled with an inexorable certainty of adequate punishment, if found guilty. These emphases affect both judicial and legislative bodies. Unfortunately, they run up against the unwillingness of states to pay for additional prisons.

The whole area of administrative law, or quasi-judicial activity, is highly fluid. As elsewhere, the crying need for new approaches to the regulation of business has resulted in a rethinking of the old assumptions.

Historically, the judiciary has had very great influence on public policy. It was the Supreme Court, for example, that decided that corporations were to be regarded as 'persons' when this term appearing in the Constitution was pertinent to a case before the Court. One historian has coined a phrase to describe the results: 'The rights of persons became the immunities of corporations.' Constitutional phrases such as the 'general welfare', 'necessary and proper', 'due process of law', or 'equal protection' are not self-defining. Neither are many legislative phrases, such as 'public interest' or 'fair and reasonable', which occur with increasing frequency in regulatory acts. The Common Law still occupies a significant place in jurisprudence, and this is judge-made law. These interstices and ambiguities in statutes and constitutions are filled in by the predilections of those who interpret them. It is not surprising, then, that at times the American judiciary has been the center of controversy in a fashion relatively unfamiliar to citizens of modern Britain. It has not been enough for a political party or an economic group to place its sympathizers in the legislature or the administration. If it would give color to the American system, the judiciary must likewise come within the orbit of political action in the broadest sense of the term.

17
The States

There are fifty partially sovereign jurisdictions dividing the territory of the United States proper.[1] While these fifty states retain relatively few functions that are still their exclusive concern, their juridical autonomy is much less seriously impaired. They constitute, therefore, a governmental laboratory of very great interest. Their sphere of action knows only the boundaries, on the one hand, of those great civil rights that Americans constitutionally have chosen to bar as spheres of any governmental action – barred to the nation as well as to the states – and on the other, of those powers over which the nation has exclusive jurisdiction. To these must be added a certain twilight zone consisting of powers in which jurisdiction is concurrent, but in which federal law prevails in the event of conflict. In the determination of the precise metes and bounds of these various limitations, the decision of the federal Supreme Court is final. The state, and not the nation, is the residuary legatee of unassigned powers. Congress may admit new states to the Union, but it cannot create them out of the territories of existing states without the latters' concurrence. The states are guaranteed a republican form of government by the federal government, and they are protected against invasion.

The states vary greatly in almost every geographic particular. In area, Alaska, the 'Great Land', with 586,400 square miles, is 483 times as large as Rhode Island, with 1,214 square miles, and 9.5 times as large as England. Two-thirds of the states range in area between 30,000 and 97,000 square miles. California, with 23,668,562 people (1980 census), has 59 times the population of Alaska, with 400,481.

New York's area is 47,944 square miles; that of Alaska is 586,400. The density of population of New Jersey is 941 people per square mile and of Alaska, .7. Almost two-thirds of the states range in population between 6,000,000 and 900,000; in density, between 260 people per square mile and 10. Forty-two have 50 per cent or more of their population living in communities over 2,500 in population. In twelve of them (Arizona, Colorado, Delaware, Hawaii, Illinois, Maryland, Massachusetts, Minnesota, New York, Nevada, Rhode Island, Utah) more than half the people live in a single metropolitan area. Those with two or more metropolitan areas over 300,000 which between them contain more than half the state's population are: California, Florida, Michigan, Missouri, New Jersey, Ohio, Pennsylvania, Tennessee, Texas, Washington.

Land characteristics vary greatly. Nevada is chiefly desert; Iowa, rich farm lands. New York, Washington, and California present extreme diversification. Colorado combines mountain and prairie. The list is practically endless.

Income and its derivative, taxable capacity, show striking differences. The per capita income of the ten poorest states (all but three of them in the South) is about 65 per cent of that of the ten wealthiest. By European standards, however, all are prosperous. The poorest, Mississippi, has a greater per capita income than Britain as a whole.

Each state has its own written constitution. These date from 1780 (Massachusetts) to 1974 (Louisiana). Almost all of them have been subjected to varying degrees of amendment. The process of framing a new constitution varies from state to state. Usually it calls for a constitutional convention, with delegates elected by the people. The draft document is usually submitted to a referendum of the people before it comes into effect. State legislatures usually propose such constitutional conventions, though in a few states the question of holding such a convention is periodically submitted to the voters. Other variants occur, such as use of a constitutional commission appointed by the governor to draft a new document.

Amendment of a constitution usually involves both the state legislature and the voters. Usually, either by extraordinary majorities or by resolutions at two consecutive sessions, the legislatures authorize the submission of amendments to the vote of the people. An alternative method in a few states is the initiative, which provides that, if a certain number of voters sign a petition to this effect, a proposed amendment is voted upon by the people. Some states require extraordinary majorities of voters for new constitutions or amendments.

State constitutions vary greatly in their length and content. Most contain a bill of rights similar to the one in the federal Constitution. Universally, they prescribe at least the main structure of the state government. Frequently, they contain a number of financial clauses, such as ones prescribing limitations of the state and local debt and even their property tax rates. Some enumerate powers of the state government, but without limiting the government to those powers enumerated. Some set up the structure of local government as well as state government, and many guarantee to local governments (especially to the cities) a sphere of constitutional autonomy outside the jurisdiction of the state legislatures. Some extend to great length, putting into the written constitution details more properly left to the field of legislation.

In broad outline, the governments set up under these state constitutions are not unlike the federal government. Except for Nebraska, which has a unicameral legislature, all the governments provide for bicameral legislatures. All provide for a governor elected by the people. Almost all give the governor a veto over legislation, but it is usually one that can be passed over by an extraordinary majority of the legislature. All provide for a system of state courts, one of whose functions is to interpret the state constitutions.

However, variants from the federal pattern are many. Except in length of a member's term and the body's size, real differentiation between the two houses of a state legislature is difficult to ascertain. Legislative terms tend to be shorter than those in the national body – two to four years for the upper house, usually two years for the lower house. The minority of legislatures meet annually, and those scheduled to meet biennially often have special sessions in the unscheduled year. Rural areas were often grossly overrepresented until recent Supreme Court decisions forced more equitable apportionment. Governors' terms are four years in a majority of states, two years in the remainder. Moreover, most of the states elect several state officials besides the governor (and lieutenant governor). Most frequently elected are the secretary of state (an officer of records, totally different from his national namesake), treasurer, comptroller, attorney general, school superintendent, and judges. A factor invalidating too glib a comparison of the position of the governor with that of the President is found in several states where the legislatures have reserved to themselves a larger measure of administrative power than has Congress. These powers often include the framing of the budget, selection of certain state officials, and detailed prescription of administrative procedure. However, during the last two or three decades, a strong movement has been in progress that advocates increasing the power and stature of the governor. In many states, his term has been lengthened, the number of departments cut down, and the exclusive appointment of department heads vested in him. Executive budgets have been installed. He has been given a veto over individual items in appropriations. His hitherto limited powers of removal of personnel have been strengthened.

About a third of the constitutions provide, in some fashion, for what is known as 'direct government'. This makes it possible for the electorate itself to vote on measures, if a sufficient number wish to do so. A certain number of signatures on a petition will either secure a chance for the people to vote on a measure which the legislature has refused or neglected to pass (the initiative), or suspend and secure a chance to vote on a measure already passed (the referendum). Although such provisions have existed for many years, informed opinion still is not ready to credit them with any very great effect for either good or ill. Use has not varied greatly over the years.

The administrative organization of the states naturally is closely correlated with the functions that the states have assumed. Sometimes state boards and bureaus are allowed to proliferate, but recent trends – and the best thought concurs – are in the direction of consolidation. We can therefore answer the questions of what the state does and how its administration is organized at the same time.

All states concern themselves with education, and this is usually their most costly function. The chief issue concerning this function in America is not between a single national system of education and state systems. It is much more a question as to whether the principle of autonomy should be carried (or allowed to remain) still further in the direction of decentralization, and local self-government in education be made or remain the guiding principle. In general, each state has a school system with certain minimum standards centrally prescribed, but with a high degree of autonomy allowed the local authorities. Subsidies to them are growing. Overseeing a state system is usually a superintendent (variously termed), and associated with him (in either an advisory or a directive capacity) a board of education. Either associated with the schools or under a separate board or official is often a state library system. Every state now maintains at least one state university, attendance at which is open to qualified resident students at moderate fees. Almost eight million are in state- and other publicly supported institutions above secondary-school level. This is over three and a third times the number in private institutions.

The field of public health, including such matters as sanitation and infant welfare, is another major aspect of state activity. Here, too, responsibility is shared with the local authorities, who usually have still more autonomy in this function than their counterparts have in education. On the other hand, extended institutional care has increasingly come to be a state, rather than a local, responsibility. Special institutions usually exist for the insane, the feeble-minded, the deaf, and often for other groups such as the epileptic. One or more state boards or officials are entrusted with these responsibilities.

Closely related are a number of other activities. Care of the aged has been revolutionized by systems of old-age pensions and insurance, with liberal federal subsidies as well as state expenditures. Correctional institutions, except in the largest cities and counties, are chiefly state-directed. State departments of recreation have established state park systems in most states.

Regulation of business, though more and more in the orbit of national interest, is still a major state function. Banks, insurance companies, corporate organizations, utilities, mines, environmental quality, land use, licensing of professions are the principal spheres of state administration and regulatory activity. The full picture would include the laws governing the day-to-day operations of business that are, for the most part, state laws enforceable in state courts. Business, on the whole, has favored state rather than federal regulation.

Organized labor, on the other hand, has sought to include in the federal orbit the regulations of chief interest to itself – wages, hours, working conditions, collective bargaining. Nevertheless a substantial residuum in these fields is left to the states, and almost all states have departments of labor. The administration of unemployment insurance is throughout the nation a state function.[2] Only family endowment, among the panoply of social insurances, is missing from the American system.

Agriculture and forestry are also in part a state responsibility. Fish and game laws are state-imposed – except that the federal government has to some extent entered this field by granting subsidies, establishing national parks and wild life refuges and wilderness areas, and even making treaties. Many states own extensive tracts of forest and park land. Texas, especially, has a very extensive and successful state land system.

Transportation represents another field of considerable state concern, shared though it is with the local authorities on the one hand and the federal government on the other. Regulation of motor vehicles and construction, maintenance, and regulation of highways are the spheres of greatest activity; but state governments play some role in railroad, canal, airport regulation, and local airlines.

A few state enterprises exist – power plants, grain elevators, canals – but these are exceptional.

Law enforcement is primarily left to the local authorities, but most states now supplement this local effort with state police forces. State militias (known as the National Guard) are also usual, and these are also tied into the national defense system.

In addition to these primary functions, each state obviously must maintain a legal department, a department of finance and taxation, and certain record offices.

Thus, the typical state administration emerges as a series of departments concerned in one fashion or another with much of the daily life of the people. Together with the local authorities, it still overshadows the federal government in this regard. Education, health, recreation, law enforcement, much of business, labor, farming, roads and highways – these are not primarily national concerns, but remain the province of the network of state and local authorities that cover the nation. Control and administration of welfare are in dispute as between state and nation.

We have already called attention to the principal aspects of federal-state relations. These have been characterized as 'cooperative federalism'. Interdependence in the case of many functions is increasingly evident, and federal subsidies are the principal lever to facilitate co-operation. The designation 'subsidy' itself is dangerous, for it may well obscure the very real element of tacit compulsion that is concealed behind the grant-in-aid. Recent figures would indicate that the states received about 43 per cent of their revenue from the federal government. Of this revenue, some was without strings, but most was earmarked for specific purposes. chiefly in welfare, education, health, and highways. These latter usually required a state to furnish a given per cent of the total. In some instances, the states were designated as 'conduits' to pass on a given per cent of the federal grants to the local units, with or without control and supervision of their use. The states made grants from this and their own tax revenues of over $36 billion to the localities. Of this about 60 per cent was for schools.

Each state is required under the federal Constitution to give full faith and credit to the acts of other states. States may enter into compacts with each other, if they are approved by Congress. These compacts are proving important devices in promoting uniform legislation and administration. They are also frequently used in connection with the allocation of water rights and in other resource development projects, and their use in joint provisions of institutional facilities is now recognized. Entirely apart from the formal device of an interstate compact, regional interstate cooperation has been a marked phenomenon in recent years. It is evident that for the best performance of many functions, states are too small and the nation is too large. Regionalism is finding modes of expression of its own in conferences and committees, often with federal representation and under federal leadership. River-valley, and port authorities, and industrial development are the chief, but by no means the only, fields of such activity.

Not so long ago, even the survival of the states as vital units was seriously called into question in the United States. This note is far less frequently heard today. The whole sphere of governmental action has been enormously extended during the present century. States, as well as the nation and the localities, have participated in this growth. In a series of decisions, the Supreme Court removed most of the judicially imposed barriers to state as well as federal action in the whole field of business regulation. The standard of living had pushed higher and higher until the recent recession. Yet more and more amenities lay within the sphere of the fiscally practicable for government to provide. While party voting has declined, enlightened public interest seems to be mounting steadily. State expenditures have grown from almost $2.8 billion in 1932 to more than $28 billion in 1958, almost $40 billion in 1963, $109 billion in 1973, and to almost $258 billion in 1981. Even when changes in purchasing power are taken into account, the gain is enormous. The quality of administration is improving intermittently, but it is improving. States' 'rights', in a constitutional sense, seem to have been impaired seriously, for few functions are any longer the exclusive concern of the states. State *vitality*, the operative reality behind the concept of states' rights, has seldom, if ever, been so great. We have noted that the system of American government puts many difficulties in the way of major forward steps on a nationwide scale through national legislative action. These difficulties become more tolerable and understandable when one appreciates how much autonomy is granted the constituent units. Otherwise frustrated groups that cannot obtain their way nationally may, in states where they can command a popular majority, try out the many proposals that are operatively practicable on this limited scale. Hence, state vitality is the parent of experiment, the precursor of national programs.

Yet, the states as laboratories cannot be the complete answer. Different taxable capacities create situations of great inequity. The national nature of many problems blocks effective state experimentation. Federal grants by category frequently set boundaries on state or local initiatives, either by regulation or necessity; as well as subsidizing the federal objectives in state and local administration. The nation gains apace, though many hold it laggard. Conversely President Reagan thinks it has gone too far! After the state governors rejected his program, they set up a committee (1982) to attempt to counter with a plan of their own. However, this initiative was soon abandoned, after agreeing with the President again to try consultation. In any event, the respective responsibilities are still left in a state of somewhat demoralizing uncertainty as between the nation, states, and localities.

President Reagan's efforts to replace grants by category with 'block grants', have had some limited success in health, social services, energy assistance for low-income recipients, and education. The numerical bulk of categorical grants still remains (early 1983). Savings of about $2.3 billion for the federal government are claimed by the Office of Management and Budget on the replacements thus far.

18
Local Government

At least until recent reforms it was usual for the British to complain about the confusion and illogic in the areas and even the types of their local authorities. They should know America better! It is not merely that the continental United States has fifty different systems of local government plus the District of Columbia. In addition, most of these fifty states have allowed a considerable measure of autonomy to their local units in the selection of their forms of government. Then also there has been even greater flexibility than in Britain in allowing 'special districts' to be formed for particular functions where a need overlaps or falls short of existing governmental jurisdictions. Moreover, education is a function that in most of the states has its own local authority independent of the other units of local government and often of their areas, as well. There are about 16,000 of these school districts, each largely autonomous. With continuing consolidation the number of school districts is decreasing. Except for Virginia and Hawaii and in a very few cities elsewhere, the quite logical separation of county and county borough which was the rule in Britain is non-existent. County government thus provides another 'layer of government' in almost all localities. Nomenclature throughout is confused.

In addition to the school districts, there are more than 62,000 other units of local government vested with a measure of local autonomy. About 3,000 of these are counties, which with rare exceptions cover the entire nation. Many of these counties in turn are subdivided into more than 18,000 incorporated cities, boroughs, and villages, and (chiefly in the North and Middle West) about 17,000 towns and townships. About

29,000 miscellaneous units, of which the most important are special districts for particular functions such as irrigation or sewage, complete the roster – a total, if school districts are included, of over 78,000 local authorities. The numbers of incorporated municipalities and special districts are increasing. The number of special districts has increased (1983) to 28,233.

If these governmental units were even laid out in a neat pattern, the picture would not be too confusing. The situation is quite otherwise. An example of what often happens is that when a built-up urban area develops, it may well cross county lines.[1] The portions within each county incorporate as one municipality, remaining, however, within their respective counties for county government purposes. One or more of them may also retain vestiges of township government. Usually the independent school districts remain, and their boundaries frequently are not identical with those of the municipalities. Then, in order to promote cooperation, perhaps for sewage disposal or water supply, one or more special districts are created, cutting across the county lines and including territory outside the two or more munici-palities. A given citizen or taxpayer finds himself subject, not only to the nation and the state, but also to the county, the special district or districts, the municipality, the school district, and possibly a township as well – in other words, to six or eight different layers of government.

Fortunately, especially in metropolitan areas, the governing bodies of many of the special districts are made up of representatives appointed by or chosen from the governing bodies of constituent local units. Under these circumstances, they form a kind of corporate board to coordinate mutual efforts, such as water or sewage disposal. Frequently, where there is not such an authority, one or more of the smaller local units will contract with a central city to furnish it certain services. Water supply, fire protection, and sewage disposal are probably the most frequently contracted for services. Indian tribes in most instances are granted a measure of autonomy within their reservations.

A less defensible reason for setting up 'special districts' has surfaced as the result of restrictive local tax laws and lessened federal aid. This is simply to avoid increasing the regular tax rate. User fees are then assessed for such services as above noted, and also including health, parks, libraries – often by a 'so-called' special district within the city.

All but two states are divided into counties,[2] which average just under 1,000 square miles in area. The population range is very great – from Loving (in Texas), with 70 people, to Los Angeles (in California), with more than 7 million. The median county population is a little over 18,000. In most states, the county government is simple and uniform – a relatively small board or council, with administrative officers either popularly elected or chosen by the council. County functions are most highly developed in the South, where health and education are often primarily a county responsibility. There and elsewhere, county functions usually include the judiciary and law enforcement, elections, highways, and welfare – but most of these are shared with the state and some with the smaller local authorities. For the most part, counties are regarded more or less as arms of the particular state, rather than as vigorous units of local self-government. Relatively speaking, the voters take little interest in them, and standards of administration are low.

In the North and most of the Middle West, the counties are still further subdivided. In New England, the 'town' is the principal unit of even rural local government, and the functions of the county are very much attenuated. A town in this sense usually comprises a village and a considerable amount of the surrounding territory. Here is the most vigorous direct democracy in America. It takes the form of the town meeting – the annual (or more frequent) meeting of all the eligible voters who care to attend – which is its governing authority. 'Selectmen', school boards, and other officials are chosen at these meetings to govern between times. Ordinances are adopted, taxes and expenditures discussed and voted upon. The reluctance of these communities to incorporate as cities is the best testimony to the satisfactory working of this system.

West of New England, but not in the South and Southwest, the township is the characteristic form of government for rural areas. Small built-up communities organize further as villages, boroughs, or even 'cities' – often without 'contracting out' of the township government. These rural or village units vary considerably in the details of their organization and the functions they administer. Usually they are governed by a small, locally-elected board, with a president, mayor, or chairman who may or may not be separately elected or vested with special powers. The board passes ordinances, selects officials, and decides upon taxes and expenditures. Local and other public improvements make up a good share of the township agenda. Usually there are separate school boards. In the villages, additional functions characteristic of built-up areas are added – lighting, health, recreation, and traffic regulation. About 2,500 locally organized and directed soil-conservation districts work in cooperation with the federal Department of Agriculture. The rural electrification cooperatives are similar in their genesis.

The most enterprising units of American local government are the cities. (In Britain, they would be called county boroughs or boroughs.) Here are very great vitality and local interests. Here also is a breadth of local discretion and self-government very much in excess of what obtains in Britain. Here also is a great variation – in quality of government, in functions undertaken, in structure.

Each city is governed under what is usually called its Charter. This is to the city what a constitution is to the state or nation. These charters are normally acquired in one of four ways. A city may ask for and receive – or receive without asking – a charter as a special act of the state legislature. The state legislature may pass general laws for all its cities, or for all its cities of a certain size, or for all its cities that have not otherwise acquired a charter. A third possibility is the optional charter – i.e., a state offers its cities several different types and allows each to choose. Finally, under what is known as 'municipal home rule', a city may frame and then adopt its own charter. These various provisions are sometimes incorporated in the state constitution, sometimes in statute law, most often in some combination of the two. Most states whose cities have 'home rule' have provided for this by incorporating the privilege in their constitutions.

The city charters themselves fall naturally into three main types – mayor-council, commission, and city manager.

The mayor-council type of city government is virtually the national and state form of government simplified. The mayor is the chief executive and is independently elected. He usually appoints most of the heads of the administrative departments. With negligible exceptions, the city council is unicameral. A few other officials may be elected. There is usually also an independently elected school board, though in a fair number of cities the board may be appointed by the mayor or chosen by the council. The council passes the ordinances, which the mayor usually may veto; it may have the power to confirm his appointments; it adopts the budget, which the mayor may or may not have formulated. In other words, division of powers between mayor and council varies, but the modern trend is in the direction of greater and greater power for the mayor. Especially where this is true, mayor-council government is apt to make for a vigorous and dynamic civic life under vigorous official leadership. It tends, however, (much more at least than the city-manager type), to be partisan and political, even in the bad sense of the latter term. Except for its utility in the very large, heterogeneous cities, it has fallen into disfavor among students of municipal administration. 44.4 per cent of the 2,439 cities over 10,000 are governed under this type of charter. This includes all but 5 of the 23 over 500,000.

The commission type, once hailed as a panacea for municipal ills, is now experiencing a steady decline in favor. In 1981 only 4.3 per cent of the cities of over 10,000 population had charters of the commission type. This charter provides for an elected commission, usually of three, five, or seven members, in whom collectively the powers of city government are vested. For purposes of administration, the commissioners divide the functions of the city by departments, and each commissioner heads a department. In practice, this often results in the creation of self-contained and uncoordinated units, and it does not provide the quality of centralized leadership a city needs.

The city-manager type has attracted worldwide attention, and has made a really outstanding contribution to the science of municipal government and administration. It is steadily gaining adherents; of the cities over 10,000 population, in 1981, 1,243, or 50.9 per cent, were under city-manager charters. It has come to be the favorite type for new adoptions in most of those states that have municipal home rule or optional charters. In general, a city-manager charter provides for a council which has three important functions: to pass ordinances, including provision for functions; to adopt a budget; and to pick a city manager. The manager holds his office at the pleasure of the council. He appoints the heads of the departments; frames the budget and presents it to the council; and makes policy recommendations to the council on request or on his own initiative. He is usually not a resident

of the city at the time of appointment but is usually a career administrator or city manager from another community. Holders of this office
have now developed their own profession, with its organization, publications, training, and code. When a city replaces its old charter with
one of this type, it almost always finds itself with a more efficient as
well as a more economical government. Partisanship, while still existing
in some city-manager cities, seldom affects the administration. Most
city-manager cities are nonpartisan in fact as well as in name. At the
same time, the council (released from the details of administration) can
give civic leadership. So also can the manager, though by tradition he
advocates nothing publicly that has not been approved by the council.
A few cities have dropped the plan, but in any one year the number of
dropouts has been far exceeded by the new adoptions. Of the 369
counties over 100,000 population, 203 have engaged 'county administrators'. Some are called 'county managers'.

In general, the functions of the American city are not dissimilar to
those of the British county borough. There is much less 'municipal
trading', but most of the other functions are perhaps even more highly
developed. For example, the average school-leaving age[3] in American
cities is higher, so the local school systems are more elaborate and
costly. A considerably higher portion of the educational expense is met
from local revenues than is the case in Britain. This is made possible
primarily by the extremely productive tax on the capital value of lands
and improvements. New York City finances 56 per cent of its revenues
(out of a total of $13,211,000,000) by local taxes and other local
resources, chiefly fees and charges for services. State and federal
governments furnish 36 per cent and 8 per cent respectively. Its
expenditures came to $13,901,000,000. These data are for 1981.

Considerable freedom is granted the American city as to the functions it undertakes and the way it performs them. The 'grants-by-
category' of the federal government, plus the latter's taxation of
potential sources of greater revenue, have, in practice, limited a city's
earlier great freedom as to the functions it undertakes and the way it
performs them. The results of the Reagan program to transfer some
additional revenues and restore greater freedom in use of remaining
federal grants, are too early to assess – particularly because most of this
program has not yet been accepted by Congress and fiscally speaking

by the states and local authorities. It is still (1983) very much in the 'negotiating stage'. On the other hand, state minimal standards for the cities, when established at all, apart from the federal grants by category, were usually voluntarily exceeded by the cities.

The metropolitan regions of the United States are farther from achieving integrated governments than are their counterparts in Britain. The number of overlapping and scattered governments makes the problem even more difficult in America than in Britain. Of its twenty-three cities over 500,000 population, only Milwaukee, Houston, Dallas, San Diego, Indianapolis, Jacksonville, Miami (?), Twin Cities (Minneapolis and St Paul), Honolulu, and New Orleans, have been reasonably successful in achieving integrated local government. This is, in fact, a worldwide problem, apparently not to be solved except by draconian measures.

If we survey local government as a whole, and more especially county, small town, and rural government, we do note a marked increase in state control of locally administered functions. The phenomenon of the central state federal subsidy is very much in evidence also in these matters. Finance, health, education, and welfare are the functions in which these trends are most marked. In general, the federal control over the use of grants to local units has been more detailed than over those to the states, even when the latter serve as conduits. Functional grants by categories are often very detailed in their controls when they reach the local level. General revenue sharing with the states is almost without strings, while the portion reaching the cities must be used in eight priority areas.

The changes in state and federal control over municipal policy have really been a reflection of two factors. First is the way in which special interests become impatient with the fiscal stringency of cities, which has reflected itself in failure of the latter to perform as the groups interested in special fields would wish. These include education, health, crime prevention, urban planning, housing, and a wide variety of other traditional local functions. This combination of group pressure for higher standards and the aforesaid stringency has resulted in a major change in financial and functional control by federal and state governments. Data for all the cities in 1980 reveal that while the locally provided financing is still the major factor (64 per cent), the federal grants now finance 14 per cent and the states 21 per cent. The corresponding figures for 1972 were 68 per cent local, 7.2 per cent federal, and 24 per cent state.

Cities, relatively speaking, are less state-controlled, more free than in Britain and American rural areas. The trend, even here, is toward state and federal influence. The Reagan administration, as already noted, is seeking to change this. Federal assistance in transportation and urban renewal springs, at least in part, from an attempt to compensate for the inadequate boundaries of the central cities in metropolitan areas, and for so many of the cities having reached the outer politically practicable limits of the property tax and other sources of local revenue. It should be borne in mind that these metropolitan areas now account for over 70 per cent of the population.

Yet, by and large, one of America's greatest achievements remains the local self-government it has succeeded in retaining in a centralizing, nationalistic age. The traditional values of differentiation, adaptation, experiment, and political education remain substantially unimpaired – and, as regards cities, they probably are increasing in effectiveness. Even where there is a loss of local freedom, it is primarily to the state government, itself a fairly small and manageable unit. Where functions are not too important, and where the unit has little sociological reality, as the county, these values are much less evident. In tone, the other principal local authorities – the towns and the cities – are not, by and large, inferior to the states, which (rather than the nation) were, at least until the recent spawning of the federal categorical grants, the alternative exercisers of discretion. A price is paid in lack of uniformity and some confusion, yet the contribution made by the experience in local self-government to a sense of responsibility in national affairs would seem to be a considerable one.

19
The American System

What then of the American *system* of government? Is there more than meets the eye in the examination of its several parts?

We have already called attention to the fact that to those accustomed to the orderly, responsible clarity of British parliamentary government, the American system carries the impression of confusion, disorder, irresponsibility, frustration, a yielding to pressures of special interests. One may grant a measure of truth to all this, but the effect, or result, or end-product seems somehow to belie this indictment of the process.

Consider the following points, some of which have already been mentioned. Of all the world's written constitutions, the American Constitution has survived the longest. Relatively speaking, it has not even been deemed necessary to amend it in any fundamental fashion. Under this Constitution, a continent has been developed. There has emerged an economy more dynamic and successful than any the world has yet seen, with government showing restraint as well as action in the control of it. The freedom of the individual and his opportunities for fulfilment of his personality are at least very much above the average among the peoples of the world, and most would give them a higher rating than this. Corruption, serious though it still is, is probably on the wane. Finally, by a series of bold strokes, this people has moved into the leadership of the free world. It is, of course, arguable that these achievements have been possible in spite of the Constitution, and certainly no one would be naive enough to claim that other factors had not made important, perhaps even more important, contributions. In the light of the extent to which the written text of the Constitution has been supplemented, interpreted, and altered by usage, one must necessarily give a share of the attendant credit or discredit to the political sense or adaptability of the people themselves. These correctives belong to the total picture.

What then, is the real essence of the American system? The accumulated evidence would justify, I think, some phrase such as this: a normal *consensus* in policy, the product of balances or equilibria in institutions, with the federal element serving as a 'safety valve'.

It is remarkable how much of the American system can be explained in these terms of balance and equilibrium; and how, taken in their collective effect, these balances result in 'government by consensus'. Only a few correctives – but these are important – have apparently been needed. We shall, therefore, review these great balances, or equilibria, one by one.

Several times, 'constitutionalism' has been mentioned as a characteristic of American political thought and behavior. By this we mean a sense that there are certain great principles and institutions in government not lightly to be changed, within the framework of which the day-to-day operations of government are to take place. The Americans have given this a very concrete application, associating it closely with their written Constitution, secondarily with the Supreme Court decisions thereunder, and then to some degree with the usages developed to supplement both of these. Two great balances are associated with the *written* nature of the Constitution: the balance between the sphere of law and the sphere of individual freedom, and the hierarchical balance between the more rigid constitutional provisions and the area of flexibility for statute law allowed thereunder.

In the balance between Constitution and statute law, there should be change only when *consensus*[1] appears – that is, when there is substantial support among all important regions and groups. The American Constitution has so responded historically. In times of crisis, this response has normally been through the utilization of the inherent but usually latent power of the President as *leader*. Then, too, through Court restraints, as well as Congressional policy, government has moved into the economic sphere only when the case was proved and consensus emerged. This allowed and still allows the dynamism of private enterprise to do its work, thus adding another balance in the field of political economy – that between state action and private capitalism.

The balance between the sphere of law and the sphere of individual freedom has served also to safeguard and develop the sphere of civil liberties, extending this concept to all classes and races as fast and as far as consensus (in this case, the mores) would allow. The underlying theory is that integration finds its principal vehicle in 'competitive' capitalism, with consumers making the ultimate choice.

The Supreme Court has viewed its function as being that of waiting for consensus to develop before removing barriers to expansion of government action. It has sought to move with the tidal forces of public opinion, and not with its waves.

Another great balance is that which lies at the heart of federalism – the balance between national action and state and local vitality. Here obviously are two principles, each of great value and great attractiveness, but frequently incompatible. Without the protection of a federal system, the almost universal experience of the great nations is that this particular equilibrium, or balance, is dangerously and fundamentally upset. The localities are defenseless against central bureaucracies confident of their own judgment and enthusiastic over their functions. They are similarly powerless against legislatures preoccupied with the national interest and subject to the pressures of economic groups who wish legislation favorable to themselves on as large a scale as possible. Their own resistance is weakened by a fiscal stringency irrelevant to the central values of their side of the balance. It has been this fact which has been largely responsible for the localities' failure to advance generally in many fields in which the national interest has been clear. Out of this has arisen the multitude of grants by category to these localities, which can only be earned if programs are introduced which correspond to national, often quite detailed, objectives. National rigidities have thereby been imposed which have not taken sufficiently into account the variations in local needs and desires.

The values of the national approach to a problem are very great, but so also is the cluster of values associated with the wide popular participation in decisions, the adaptation, the experiment, which are really possible only in situations of vigorous local self-government. It is the very genius of a federal system that these values are not to be invaded or weakened lightly, even in the interest of other values; and the genius of the American system has, at least till recently, been that this is not to take place at all until consensus appears. Reagan has thrown his weight in the direction of restoration of greater local vitality.

The American system has been adjudged most vulnerable in the power that seems to be held by special interests. In part, this particular indictment undoubtedly arises from the fact that the American system tends to subject these pressures by special interests to a considerably greater publicity, especially to the publicity that attends investigation and controversy, than is the fact in many other nations. Yet there is far too much truth in the indictment for Americans to be at all complacent.

On the other hand, an essential truth is missed if the issue is always phrased in the terms of 'pressure groups versus the public interest'. Looked at in another way, what is sought is rather a balance between pluralism and unity. Pluralism has usually been defined in more strictly political terms: as a type of government that is made up of several freely functioning centers of power, as geographic local self-government, or as a series of 'authorities' for various aspects of economic and social life. What we mean, at this point, by the term is a special adaptation of the last, in which power is still further diffused, and in which the principal characteristic of society and economy is the proliferation of groups, subgroups, and organizations, each with very considerable autonomy. In the economic sphere, especially in a primarily competitive capitalism, this has a vitality akin to that of local self-government. The 'unity' with which this must achieve 'balance' consists in the *integrating of the results*. Now this economic pluralism of today is a species of 'group utilitarianism'. The original Utilitarians – Bentham and his followers – believed that each individual was the best judge of his own welfare, and therefore that that government was best which least interfered with individual freedom. The 'group utilitarianism' of the present day assumes that each group – banking, mining, steel, labor, medicine, agriculture, and the innumerable subdivisions – knows what is best for itself and that these bests add up to the common good. Each, therefore, asks from government that which it believes will bring it the most benefit. Unlike the early Utilitarians, however, these groups do not seek nonintervention so much as intervention – intervention on behalf of each group in the economic struggle.

The balance to be sought in government is, therefore, really a balance between the vitality of these economic groups and their integration. In the 1930s, it seemed as though the United States (like Weimar Germany, pre-Fascist Italy, and the Fourth French Republic) was becoming almost too dispersive to survive. Except during the crisis of war or near-war, the lack of integrating factors has been the American Government's greatest weakness. It still is terribly dangerous despite the gradual emergence of embryo integrating institutions in the Presidency and Congress. This balance is still to be achieved, but it is a *balance* that is to be achieved, and not the paralysis of economic vitality which would accompany a completely planned or integrated society.

One notes also in the American system a balance between partisanship and independence – that is, between organizational responsibility with its necessary compromises and the moral and intellectual integrity of the individual. Among the voters, the latter expresses itself in voting for the man on the basis of his character and ability rather than for the party – but with party organizations sufficiently strong to bring forward candidates and espouse principles and hence present meaningful choices. In the national government (and to a considerable extent in state governments), it finds its chief expression in the field of policy adoption, whereby the parties assume the responsibility for organized consideration and criticism, but the end result depends upon consensus among the individuals in both the executive and Congress. The independently elected, fixed-term executive is probably what makes this particular equilibrium practicable, though the Swiss system of a permanent bureaucratic executive and the former Uruguayan committee government have somewhat similar potentialities.

But the heart of the problem of attaining the consensus produced by balance of forces lies in the relationship between the executive and Congress. In Britain, the executive (the Cabinet) must defend its course before Parliament, but it can also usually override Parliament through its power of dissolution and its party discipline, even if its defense of its position fails to convince. In the American system, it must not only defend, it must also convince – and convince in such a fashion that the conviction represents consensus.

On this point, as well as for all of this concluding chapter, I must add a word of caution. There are exceptions to almost all these generalizations. Moreover, there are considerable variations in degree of truth, accounted for by the variables of crisis, personalities, subject matter. It is of the essence of an equilibrium that it is, in a measure, unstable, subject to disturbance one way or the other. But it is also of its essence that, like a pendulum, it contains within it corrective elements that are set in motion by its disturbance. The American system at its heart has equipped each of the two in the various pairs of balance elements with reserves of power which permit a reassertion after temporary yielding. The system is flexible and supple, but the more the flexibility is strained, the greater the force making for a restoration of balance.

To return to the balance between Congress and the executive: we summarize this by rephrasing an idea that we have mentioned a number of times. Throughout the American Constitution and the usages developed thereunder are found numerous institutions that (in the present-day context) insist that centers of power justify themselves before their constitutional (and *de facto*) equals. This justification must include policy in its various aspects. Real conviction, not merely assent, must result. Note in this connection the following institutions: the veto power of the President; bicameralism; the role of the House Rules Committee; filibuster in the Senate; Congressional investigations; the independence of members of Congress; Presidential appointments and Senate confirmation thereof; the treaty-making process; executive agreements that require either legislation or appropriations to be effective; the President's power as commander-in-chief and the Congressional power to make rules for the armed services; the technical competence of the staffs of Congress as well as of the executive; the dramatic appeal of the President.

These and other factors of only relatively lesser importance add up to the requirement of effective justification at the policy level in both Presidential and Congressional activity. Liaison devices – party, patronage, conferences – do much to facilitate the workability of the system. In sudden crises, this system has shown adaptability, especially through full use of the implied powers of the executive – but through either Court action or subsequent reassertion of the Congressional role, the balance has been restored.

Congressional initiative, usually arising from investigations and hearings and (especially in foreign affairs) from debate, finds itself up against the veto or the use of various executive powers, after study by the departments. Presidential leadership requires ratification, even in most decisions in foreign policy. The end result, in spite of much controversy (more in public than in private), is normally a high degree of cooperation on the part of equals to achieve that end result best in the public interest.

We turn finally to certain over-all conclusions.

First, because of (*a*) the looseness of party ties and discipline and the growth of independence, (*b*) the strength of regional and state vitality, (*c*) the minority position of any *one* special interest (agriculture in the Senate is a possible exception), (*d*) the attitude of the Supreme Court, and (*e*) above all, separation of powers, a major change requires consensus as we have defined it.

Secondly, this consensus is made more tolerable because most major changes of policy in the emotionally charged economic and social spheres need not wait for national consensus in those states in which such changes can command a state majority, but may be instituted there once such a majority appears.

In the third place, the Americans are a volatile people, often passing rapidly from one extreme to another. They are a polyglot people with fluid and contradictory sentiments and standards. They are intense in the emotional content they assign to certain issues. With such a people, 'built-in' restraints against too rapid action and against the intolerance of temporary majorities are peculiarly valuable. Their Constitution gives these.

In the fourth place, the multiplicity of governmental institutions; the diffusion of decisions geographically and institutionally; and the pluralism in government, economy, and society all result in tremendous discussion and activity. This takes place in a situation of *balances*, but the balances are sufficiently flexible to adjust themselves to demonstrated need. Americans are politically articulate, and they are acquiring political maturity – in part as a by-product of their basic pragmatism.

We may then say that among the peculiar contributions made to representative government by the American Constitution are at least the following:

1 Orderly progress, without sharp class division.
2 The vitality of the lesser units of government.
3 Adaptation to a multiplicity of issues, without surrender of integrity of intellect or conscience.
4 Retention of the reality of elected representation in a technical and specialized age.

All this has been said without calling attention to the role of ethical and spiritual factors. In the end, these must have the final word in any working institution such as government, where motive and meaning are decisive for success or failure. No democracy can succeed unless it has among its people its necessary share of regard for individual rights, a sense of obligation to participate in promoting the public interest, a willingness on the part of groups to forget their selfish ends for a demonstrated common good, and an integrity in discussion. Some, unconscious of their largely religious origin, possess these virtues in large measure. Others, however, are more consciously inspired by a living faith that government is not the least of the agencies through which may be built the Kingdom of God among the free.

Suggested Further Reading

The titles that follow are only a few of the many that might be mentioned. They have been chosen in part because they are up-to-date, in part because they supplement the approach used in this work. The books are classified according to the chapter in this book that they supplement.

1 Introduction

Burns, James M., and Peltason, Jack W., *Government by the People*, 8th ed. Englewood Cliffs, N.J., Prentice-Hall, 1978.
Carr, Robert K., et al., *Essentials of American Democracy*, 7th ed. Hinsdale, Ill., Dryden Press, 1977.

2 The Written Constitution

Bickel, Alexander M., *The Supreme Court and the Idea of Progress*. New York, Harper and Row, 1978.
Dewey, Donald O., *Union and Liberty: A Documentary History of American Constitutionalism*. New York, McGraw-Hill, 1969.
Mason, Alphaus T., and Leach, Richard H., *In Quest of Freedom*, 2nd ed. Englewood Cliffs, N.J., Prentice-Hall, 1972.

3 The Nation and the States

Walker, David B., *Toward a Functioning Federalism*. Cambridge, Mass., Winthrop, 1981.
Wright, Beil S., *Understanding Intergovernmental Relations*, 2nd ed. Monterey, Calif., Brooks-Cole, 1982.

4 Congress: Its Organization and Election

Griffith, Ernest S., and Valeo, Francis R., *Congress: Its Contemporary Role*, 5th ed. New York, New York University Press, 1975.
Mann, Thomas E., and Orstein, Norman J. (eds.), *The New Congress*. Washington, DC, American Enterprise Institute, 1981.

5 Congress: Its Procedure

Galloway, George B., *The Legislative Process in Congress*. New York, Thomas Y. Crowell, 1953.
Riddick, Floyd M., *Enactment of a Law*. Washington, DC, Government Printing Office, 1967.

6 How Congress Makes Up Its Mind

Clapp, Charles L., *The Congressman*. Washington, DC, The Brookings Institution, 1963.
Lowi, Theo J., and Ripley, Randall B., *Legislative Politics*, USA 3rd ed. Boston, Little, Brown, 1973.
Polsby, Nelson W., *Political Promises*. New York, Oxford University Press, 1974.

7 The Chief Executive

Corwin, Edward S., *The President: Office and Powers*, 4th ed. New York, New York University Press, 1957.
Koenig, Louis W., *The Chief Executive*, 3rd ed. New York, Harcourt, Brace and World, 1976.

8 The Presidency

Cronin, Thomas E., and Greenberg, Sanford D. (eds.), *The Presidential Advisory System*. New York, Harper and Row, 1969.
Cronin, Thomas E., *State of the Presidency*. Boston, Little, Brown, 1980.
James, Dorothy B., *The Contemporary Presidency*, 2nd ed. Indianapolis, Ind., Bobbs-Merrill, 1974.
Griffith, Ernest S., *The American Presidency*. New York, New York University Press, 1976.

9 The Bureaucracy

Davis, James W., Jr., *The National Executive Branch*. New York, Free Press, London, Collier-MacMillan, 1970.
Woll, Peter, *American Bureaucracy*, 2nd ed. New York, W. W. Norton, 1977.
Heclo, Hugo, *A Government of Strangers*. Washington, DC, The Brookings Institution, 1979.

10 The Control of the Executive

Fisher, Louis, *President and Congress*. New York, Free Press, 1972.
Griffith, Ernest S., and Valeo, Francis R., *op. cit.*
Sundquist, James L., *The Decline and Resurgence of Congress*. Washington, DC, The Brookings Institution, 1981.

11   The Sources of Public Policy

Truman, David B., *The Governmental Process: Political Interests and Public Opinion*, 2nd ed. New York, Alfred A. Knopf, 1971.
Gross, Bertram, *Friendly Fascism*. New York, M. Evans, 1980.

12   Finance and Fiscal Policy

Schick, Allen, *Congress and Money*. Washington, DC, Urban Institute, 1981.
Fenno, Richard E., *The Power of the Purse*. Boston, Little, Brown, 1966.

13   The Instruments of International Policy

Estes, Thomas S., and Lightner, E. Allen, Jr., *The Department of State*. New York, Praeger Publishers, 1976.
Kissinger, Henry A., *American Foreign Policy*. New York, W. W. Norton, 1977.
Lerche, Charles O., Jr., *Foreign Policy of the American People*, 3rd ed. Englewood Cliffs, N.J., Prentice-Hall, 1967.

14   Defense in a Nuclear Age

Head, Richard G., and Rokke, Erwin J. (eds.), *American Defense Policy*, 3rd ed. Baltimore and London, Johns Hopkins University Press, 1973.
Kintner, William R., and Foster, Richard B. (eds.), *National Strategy in a Decade of Change*. Lexington, Mass., D. C. Heath, 1973.

15   Political Parties

Key, V. O., Jr., *Politics, Parties and Pressure Groups*, 5th ed. New York, Thomas Y. Crowell, 1964.
Sundquist, James L., *Dynamics of the Party System*. Washington, DC, The Brookings Institution, 1973.
Schaffer, William R., *Party and Ideology in the United States Congress*. Lanham, Md., University Press of America, 1980.

16   The Judiciary

Mason, Alpheus T., and Beaney, William M., *The Supreme Court in a Free Society*. New York, W. W. Norton, 1968.
McCloskey, Robert G., *The Modern Supreme Court*. Cambridge, Mass., Harvard University Press, 1972.

17   The States

Adrian, Charles R., *State and Local Government*, 3rd ed. New York, McGraw-Hill, 1976.
Feld, Richard D., and Grafton, Carl (comps.), *The Uneasy Partnership*, Palo Alto, Calif., National Press Books, 1973.

Morehouse, Sarah M., *State Politics, Parties and Policy*. New York, Holt, Rinehart and Winston, 1981.

18 Local Government

Adrian, Charles R., *Governing Urban America*, 4th ed. New York and London, McGraw-Hill, 1977.
Torrence, Susan W., *Grass Roots Government* [County]. Washington DC, Robert B. Luce, 1974.
Peterson, Paul E., *City Limits*. Chicago, University of Chicago Press, 1981.

Notes

1 Introduction

1 See p. 146.

2 This term will be used throughout for want of a better one. 'Consensus' requires that there be an over-all majority composed in the fashion mentioned. The concept of 'concurrent majorities' is not the same, for this assumes actual majorities in *each* major region or group. This latter concept was propounded in the first half of the nineteenth century by John C. Calhoun, a Southern statesman concerned, among other things, with preserving slavery and free trade for the South in spite of the opposition of a majority in the North and West.

2 The Written Constitution

1 See Merrill Jensen, *The New Nation* (New York, Alfred A. Knopf, 1950), for the history of the period.

2 For the development of this thesis, see Charles A. Beard, *An Economic Interpretation of the Constitution of the United States* (New York, Macmillan Co., 1935).

3 The Twenty-first Amendment (1933), repealing prohibition, was submitted to conventions in the several states.

3 The Nation and the States

1 *Ware v. Hilton*, 3 Dallas 199 (USA 1796).

2 *Clarke v. Harwood*, 3 Dallas 342 (USA 1795).

3 Constitution, Article I, Section 10; *Fletcher v. Peck*, 6 Cranch 139 (USA 1810).

4 *United States v. Fisher*, 2 Cranch 358 (USA 1805); *McCulloch v. Maryland*, 4 Wheaton 410 (USA 1819).

5 *McCulloch v. Maryland*, 4 Wheaton 404 (USA 1819).

6 *McCulloch v. Maryland*, 4 Wheaton 426 (USA 1819).

7 Cf. pp. 157, 158.

8 Note the explicit statement in *United States v. Butler*, 297 USA 1 (1939). It had been implicit in earlier decisions.

9 Edward S. Corwin (ed.), *Constitution of the United States: Analysis and Interpretation* (Washington, DC, Government Printing Office, 1953 ed.), p. xiv.

10 Cf. Chapter 17.

4 Congress: Its Organization and Election

1 Article I, Section 7, Clause 1. This gave the House the initial role in revenue bills. Usage has added appropriation bills.

2 Article II, Section 2, Clause 2. Two-thirds of the Senators present must concur in a treaty ratification.

3 ibid. Confirmation of appointments is by majority vote. Congress may exempt from this provision such employees as it desires.

4 See Article I, Section 2, Clause 5 and Section 3, Clause 6 for details. See also p. 93 below.

5 1980 Census. Also elsewhere unless specified.

6 Exceptions are too rare to deserve mention.

7 The term coined when the shape of such a partisan-arranged district in Massachusetts was found to resemble a salamander. It came to be called a 'Gerrymander' after the politician chiefly responsible for it.

8 *Wesberry v. Sanders*, 376 USA 1 (1964).

9 Article I, Section 2, Clause 2; Section 3, Clause 3. They shall be 'inhabitant(s) when elected'.

10 ibid.

11 This lies within the power of each state to determine.

12 Cf. Chapter 15.

13 This is a relatively recent development. The last of those who used their power ruthlessly for party ends was Speaker Joseph Cannon, who held the office from 1903 to 1911.

5 Congress: Its Procedure

1 At its discretion subject to certain provisions for overruling, the Rules Committee decides when a bill is to receive floor consideration; how long a debate is to be allowed, including debate on amendments; whether, in fact, amendments may be offered from the floor, and how the time is to be controlled. Favorable rules may be made conditional upon inclusion by the sponsoring committee of amendments desired by the Rules Committee.

2 This is by no means synonymous with 'minority party' or the British 'Opposition'; it usually means the opponents (regardless of party) of a measure favorably reported by a committee, and this may or may not be along party lines (cf. pp. 53*ff.*).

6 How Congress Makes Up Its Mind

1 Cf. p. 152*f.*

2 Ernest S. Griffith and Francis R. Valeo, *Congress: Its Contemporary Role* (5th ed., New York, New York University Press, 1975), p. 148.

7 The Chief Executive

1 For Thomas Jefferson in 1801 and John Quincy Adams in 1825.
2 Cf. Chapter 15.
3 Once in a while, a voter may, in certain states, 'split' his vote for electors, perhaps in order to give a complimentary vote to a particular elector. On rare occasions, this has resulted in a divided electoral vote. Also, in 1960 and in 1964, certain Southern electors declined to be bound by the national party choice.
4 The Democrats held the Presidency continuously from 1933 to 1953.
5 See p. 148.
6 For the history of this period, see Carl B. Swisher, *American Constitutional Development* (Boston, Houghton Mifflin Co., 1954), pp. 278*ff*. Chief Justice Taney attempted unsuccessfully to uphold habeas corpus over military courts.
7 For the Nixon presidency, see pp. 72, 99, 116.
8 Dean Rusk, 'The President', *Foreign Affairs*, April 1960, p. 369.

8 The Presidency

1 Cf. p. 136.
2 Note that the Office of Personnel Management has responsibilities considerably wider than its British counterpart. These include, not only recruiting, but also classification, retirement, welfare, and personnel matters generally. The Director is a presidential appointment and thus not necessarily a 'career man'.
3 *Center for the Study of the Presidency*, Vol. III, No. 1, Ch. VI. (New York, 1980).

9 The Bureaucracy

1 See pp. 99*f*.
2 Cf. Peter Woll, *American Bureaucracy* (New York, W. W. Norton, 1963), for a brilliant presentation of this thesis.
3 The Act was re-enacted several times, and its latest extension was until 1980.
4 Some of the nominees were from private life.

10 The Control of the Executive

1 Forbidden activities include the solicitation of political contributions, active campaigning, and use of authority for political purposes.

11 The Sources of Public Policy

1 Ernest S. Griffith, *The Impasse of Democracy* (New York, Harrison-Hilton, 1939), p. 182.
2 Cf. Alison Griffith, *The National Aeronautics and Space Act of 1958* (Washington, DC, Public Affairs Press, 1962).

12 Finance and Fiscal Policy

1 The small estimates for the legislative establishment are sent to the Office of

Management and Budget for procedural convenience, but they may not be altered by the Office.

2 Cf. p. 73 for a description of this Office.

13 The Instruments of International Policy

1 *The President: Office and Powers* (3rd ed., New York, New York University Press, 1948), p. 208.
2 See p. 72.
3 Consultation took place also both before and after the years the Senator was Chairman – that is, also during the time when he was ranking minority member.
4 See the annual series of *Committee Prints* entitled *Congress and Foreign Policy* (Washington, DC, Government Printing Office, var.).

15 Political Parties

1 Probably more than is strictly warranted, if we take into account 'inclinations' toward one party or the other.
2 See p. 127.
3 Until 1959, California had a system known as 'cross-filing', whereby the same man might enter the direct primary of both parties. These primaries are the most frequent way in which candidates are selected. In most states, a voter is supposed to vote only in the primary of his own party.
4 The Dixiecrats represented the faction among the Southern Democrats in 1948 that bolted the party because of strenuous objections to the Truman attitude toward race relations. Mississippi chose unpledged electors in 1960, and was joined by Alabama in 1964.

16 The Judiciary

1 *Marbury v. Madison*, 1 Cranch 137 (USA 1803).
2 *Dred Scott v. Sandford*, 19 Howard 393 (USA 1857).
3 Cf. p. 16.
4 *Brown v. Board of Education*, 347 US 483 (1954); *Brown v. Board of Education*, 349 US 294 (1955); *Mayor v. Dawson*, 350 US 877 (1950); *Gayle v. Browder*, 352 US 903 (1956).
5 Cf. p. 78*f*.

17 The States

1 Plus the federal District of Columbia – a territorial anomaly.
2 Federal subsidies are forthcoming only if a state has acceptable standards of administration.

18 Local Government

1 At times, it may cross state lines as well. There are also certain other anomalies. New York City includes five counties. Many villages also are subject to township government.

2   The equivalent term in Louisiana is 'parish'.

3   A voluntary rather than a compulsory age: most pupils stay on after the compulsory age is reached. This varies from 14 to 18, according to the state. Sixteen is most usual, though work permits are granted in many states earlier than this if the student has met certain standards.

19   The American System

1   The author is again conscious of the inappropriateness of the word 'consensus' and hence the need to define it. We repeat that Calhoun's 'concurrent majorities', which is somewhat akin to it, is, however, sharply inaccurate, because actual majorities of each group and region are not required for the type of consensus here understood. What is required is a *general* majority in which all major regions and groups are substantially represented.

Index